MOURNING

KATRINA

A POETIC RESPONSE TO TRAGEDY

MOURNING
KATRINA

A POETIC RESPONSE TO TRAGEDY

Edited by Joanne V. Gabbin

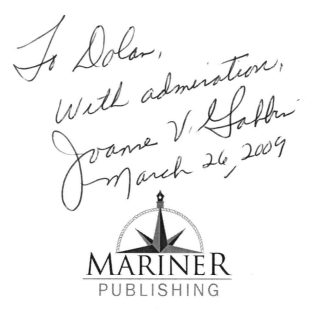

To Dolan,
With admiration,
Joanne V. Gabbin
March 26, 2009

MARINER
PUBLISHING

Library of Congress Control Number: 2008938664
Mourning Katrina: A Poetic Response to Tragedy
Edited by Joanne V. Gabbin

p. cm.

1.   American Poetry — 21st Century
2.   African American Poetry — 21st Century

I. Gabbin, Joanne V. 1946—   II. Title
ISBN 13: 978-0-9800077-8-7 (softcover : alk. paper)
ISBN 13: 978-0-9800077-9-4 (casebound : alk. paper)

1 3 5 7 9 10 8 6 4 2

Book design by Jennifer Law Young
Photography by James Madison University faculty, students and staff
Cover: original art by Christopher Johnson

Mariner Publishing
A division of
Mariner Media, Inc.
131 West 21st St.
Buena Vista, VA 24416
Tel: 540-264-0021
http://www.MarinerMedia.com
Printed in the United States of America

This book is printed on acid-free paper meeting the requirements of the American Standard for Permanence of Paper for Printed Library Materials.

The Compass Rose and Pen are trademarks of Mariner Media, Inc.

Dedicated to the survivors of Hurricane Katrina.

To all those who assisted the victims of the storm in their time of need.

To the memory of all those who died as a result of Hurricane Katrina and to their families who are left to mourn their loss.

CONTENTS

I. And the Children Shall Lead Them

II. History in the Water

III. My Soul Is Anchored

Preface

Our most immediate twentieth-century literary references for beginning to appreciate how poetic response to tragedy navigates life are writings that bear witness to such mega-tragedies as the histories of the long and obscene enslavement of African peoples on several continents and the Holocaust. As we read the literature of slavery and the literature of genocide, we are reading simultaneously two sides of the currency to be found in the dynamics of natural disasters and unnatural, man-created disasters that lend specificity to the amoral phenomena of Nature. These writings are inscriptions of human spirit and reason, the primal resilience of woman and man; they properly belong to an aesthetic of necessity. They function also to help us not to forget that human beings are exceptionally fragile in cosmic schemes, at once victims and authors of tragedy.

As we experience and interpret expressions in the aftermath of Hurricanes Katrina and Rita, we sense the human body in pain, the articulation of wounds compounded by the prior trauma of 9/11 and the implosion of symbols of power. The poems, or individual configurations of language, in *Mourning Katrina: A Poetic Response to Tragedy* recall for us certain associative powers of the human mind, our capacities for dealing with things as modern as existentialism and the Absurd and things as ancient as religious beliefs and hope that healing shall eventually manifest itself. For those of us so privileged as to have endured and survived disasters, these poems offer possibilities for removal from and reflection on the actuality of tragedy. They are instances of meaning rather than species of generic supplements for meaning.

Given the complex nature of contemporary poetics, the work in this book gives rise to Sankofa moments of our dwelling with language, including the language of advanced mass media which desperately seeks to frame and fix our understandings of what reality might be. The poems are opportunities to look forward and backward in a single motion, to survey (either consciously or not so consciously) where a poem comes from, what it can accomplish, and how it augurs a future. Readers steeped in poetic theory shall recall William Wordsworth's pontifications regarding association of "ideas in a state of excitement" and how "language really used by men," especially in the lower frequencies of life, might promote a reincorporation of human passions "with the beautiful and permanent forms of nature." There is anguish in recognizing that natural disasters such as Katrina are permanent but not beautiful; that despite the need to have romance and brief joy in the midst of tragedies, Wordsworth's Romantic dream is an unfit remedy for what ails us post-Katrina. What serves our interests best and is prominent in the strongest works in this anthology are poems that approach the critical realism implicit in the poetics of Walt Whitman or Amiri Baraka. Our bodies and minds and places of habitation need poems that can assist us in radical restoration.

The presentation of some of the work in *Mourning Katrina: A Poetic Response to Tragedy* as a combination of the spoken word with gospel music was exceptionally effective on the CD "My Soul is Anchored: Poems from the Mourning Katrina National Writing Project" (2006) issued by the Furious Flower Poetry Center. Thus, one way to get the sound/meaning of the poems into one's head as a catalyst for productive action is to read against or in concert with music. I would especially recommend Terence Blanchard's CD "A Tale of God's Will (a requiem for Katrina)" *[Blue Note Records 0946 3 91532 20, 2008]*.

In *Collapse: How Societies Choose to Fail or Succeed* (2005), Jared Diamond wrote eloquently of the lessons we should learn from previous environmental disasters and the chosen responses, particularly those driven by the politics of capitalism. Likewise, this collection of works by neophytes and master poets is a series of eloquent lessons about humanity and cultures. Scrutinize and absorb the pages. Learn.

Jerry W. Ward, Jr.
New Orleans

Introduction

   This collection of poems, *Mourning Katrina: A Poetic Response to Tragedy*, was born out of human suffering, the experience and the perception of it. During the first few days of the Hurricane Katrina disaster--when the extent of the destruction was still being gauged and those spared the initial onslaught of the Category 4 hurricane were seeking refuge in the Superdome and Convention Center in New Orleans and shelters all over the Gulf Coast--I saw a little boy on CNN. He was pleading to the person holding the camera, "We need some help here. We need food. We need water. There's a lady over there that doesn't have her medicine. She will die without it. Please help." His pleas for assistance touched the very core of my conscience as an American citizen.

   Sorely aware of the promises of preceding generations concerning freedom and the value of human life, I was ashamed that children and adults were being herded into spaces that were ill-equipped to handle the numbers needing shelter. I was shocked and angry that local, state, and national agencies were slow to coordinate their efforts to help rescue those stranded and to save lives. Though I could not have known the full extent of the devastation and the loss of life at that time, I was convinced that those who survived this storm would need a way to express the trauma that they had experienced and those of us who witnessed this human tragedy would need a way to express our feelings of helplessness and rage.

   In his book *Southern Road* (1932), poet Sterling Brown captured in his portrait of blues singer Ma Rainey, a woman who knew about the suffering of those who survived the 1927 Mississippi flood. He was able to show Ma Rainey's effect on those who heard her sing "Back Water Blues " and how she could wring from their pain a gritty perseverance and transcendence:

I talked to a fellow an' the fellow say,
"She jes'catch hold of us, somekindaway,
She sang Backwater Blues one day:
    'It rained fo' days an' de skies was dark as night,
    Trouble taken place in de lowlands at night.

    Thundered an' lightened an' the storm begin to roll
    Thousan's of people ain't got no place to go.

    "Den I went an' stood upon some high ol' lonesome hill,
    An' looked down on the place where I used to live.'

An' den de folks, dey natchally bowed dey heads an' cried,

Bowed dey heavy heads, shet dey moufs up tight an' cried,

An' Ma lef' de stage, an' followed some de folks outside."

Dere wasn't much more de fellow say:
She jes' gits hold of us dataway.
                    (Brown, *Southern Road,* 64)

In the aftermath of Hurricane Katrina, many of us
have turned to recordings of Bessie Smith, who originally
recorded "Back Water Blues," as a way to transcend the pain
that resulted from the 2005 flood. And some of us have
become writers of poetry.

In reality, more than 1800 people died as a result
of the storm, and 1.3 million people lost their homes. Some
were forced to start again in other sections of the country.
Others had to rebuild their homes on the Gulf Coast with
little assistance from FEMA and often in opposition to
corporate speculators and governmental agencies that had
other ideas for the land that used to be their homes and
communities. More than 225,000 jobs were eliminated, and
90,000 square miles, an area larger than Great Britain, were
affected. Now three years after Hurricanes Katrina and Rita

hit the Gulf Coast, many of the devastated areas in Louisiana and Mississippi have not been cleared and infrastructures are still lacking. The physical effects of this storm are readily apparent; however, the emotional and psychological problems that Hurricane Katrina victims have experienced may last long after the physical structures are repaired and rebuilt. According to Loretta Silva, a trauma specialist in the psychiatry department at Wake Forest University, a large number of Hurricane Katrina victims can be expected to develop post-traumatic stress disorder that persists for the rest of their lives (*Charlotte Observer* 19 September 2005: B3). These survivors continue to be at risk, not only of emotional trauma, but of the accompanying violence, substance abuse, and family disintegration associated with anxiety. According to the National Association of School Psychologists, children are especially susceptible to post-disaster stress and anxiety disorders because they have not developed the coping skills of adults. Hurricane Katrina created almost all of the elements associated with child post-traumatic anxiety: survivor guilt, strong sights and sounds, including seeing dead and decomposing bodies, loss of pets, relocation, and weakened family support. Existing risk factors, such as poverty and deprivation, increase the likelihood of post-disaster emotional problems (29 November 2005<www.nasp.org).

Because of my strong belief in the healing power of words, on September 5, 2005, I launched the "Mourning Katrina" project, under the auspices of the Furious Flower Poetry Center at James Madison University. It was designed to be a national writing project to which those affected by the devastation of the hurricane could respond. The rationale for the writing project was simple: after the victims of the hurricane have received those things necessary for life and have been reunited with their families, they will need to respond to the horrific events that have changed their lives forever; they will go through the process of grieving, reflection, expression and ultimately healing. The act of writing, we hoped, would aid the healing process. We sent blank writing booklets to poets and teachers from around the country and asked them to distribute the booklets at evacuation centers, schools, churches and other sites on the Gulf Coast. Several of them--including Marvin Broome, Daryl Cumber Dance, Toi Derricotte, Miriam DeCosta-Willis, Trudier Harris, Tony Medina, jessica care moore, Opal Moore, Tiwanna Simpson, and Jerry Ward--also agreed to read the poetic responses that were mailed in to the Furious Flower Poetry Center and write back to those who submitted the poems.

In all, more than 200 people participated in the project. Many were young people who had never submitted a poem or narrative before. One such person, college student Brittney Sherrod, in relating her fears during the first hours of the disaster wrote, "I wasn't at home when the hurricane came through my town, but my parents were. I worried so much about them because there was no way for me to contact them. I cried and cried until I realized that crying wasn't going to get me anywhere, so I prayed." Some were adults who had never thought to submit a poem about anything but felt compelled to break their silence in an effort to give expression to this tragedy that uncovered America in such a profound way. Tori Omega Arthur prefaced her entry with this note:

> Three days ago, a dear friend forwarded to me your email plea for poetic responses to the Hurricane Katrina tragedy. "You should send your Katrina poem here," she wrote. My initial response was, "No, I am not a poet. I will not offend the folks at Furious Flower with my frustrated rambles." But in the last three days, I've grown to understand that the frustrated rambles of poets and "non-poets" will keep the spirit of the disaster and our government's disappointing response fresh in our nation's psyche. The frustrated rambles of those directly and indirectly affected have the power to shape the way our nation views the treatment of and treats its

underprivileged citizens and its citizens of color. And, those frustrated rambles have the power to help those still reeling emotionally, financially, and spiritually from this tragedy.

Bruce Baker, another contributor to this collection, sums up the significance of all the poems in *Mourning Katrina:* "The poems are a personal rendering of the storm's impact on our social journey as a people who held fast to the voices of those that preceded them." They are, he continues, "a metaphorical account of how we can juxtapose the physical manifestation of a terrible storm with human suffering." Jerry Ward, himself an evacuee from New Orleans and contributor to this volume, allows us to sense the violence of this natural disaster and how it severely changed his life in this passage from "October 30, 2005: Covering and Recovering at Grinnell College" that he wrote during his own exile from New Orleans:

> The taste of bitter tonic is heavy on my tongue. I must face the violence as certainly as the criminal must face the music here or hereafter. Violence, you are the cause of death, the cause of rot and stench and sickness. You are a primal agent in the creation of debris. You murder dreams. You kick hope in its ribs. You sponsor projects of emotional wreckage. You engender tears, trauma, curses, the dreadful thought that the Almighty was taking a nap when the violence of a natural disaster occurred.

Perhaps the most poignant voices in this volume are those of the children who range in age from eight to seventeen. For most of them it is their first experience with writing a poem. We hear them finding strength and meaning in their memories of the calmer, happier days before Hurricane Katrina hit. Sherice King writes, "Cry me a river and I'll give you a waterfall/filled with hope to cancel out all the pictures/painted by the unstoppable storm..." These children have not yet learned the subtleties of guile or lost their innocence to experience. In "Water Line," ten-year-old Rowan Gryder cuts to the core to reveal the shameful economic divide in America with his articulation of "a line that separates circumstance." Their observations, like those of fifteen-year-old Libby Ingram, are often fresh and insightful. She observes, "Mold and dirt climb the once decorated walls like dense jungle vines" in her poem "Cleaning off Katrina." As we would expect, their messages are ones of hope and faith in the future. In a poem called "Destruction," Glen Buck, who was 16 years old when he submitted this poem, voices the determination and resolve that have become emblematic of so many residents of New Orleans who plan to continue the legacy of their famous city:

> She changed our land but not our way
> The food, the jazz and Mardi Gras parades.
> We'll still be here dancing and having fun
> She may have hurt but she has not won.

These poems by first-time writers, featured in the section titled "The Children Shall Lead Us," have the immediacy and relevance of survivor narratives. They lead us to the scenes of destruction and the tangle of uprooted lives.

This volume also contains the poems of seasoned poets. Their poems have depth and complexity and unleash a flood of ironies, invective, and witness. In the section titled "History in the Water," the poems overflow with the backwash of centuries of oppression and injustice and the toxicity of current politics. Angela Jackson, in her poem "The Last Door," sets up a striking comparison between the door at Goree's Slave House and the way the Hurricane Katrina survivors walked out of the flood:

> The Last Door, out of fetid, dank darkness
> out of the flood
>
> seeping under
> into our shabby shoes

until we walk
a ragged step
like people in shackles
but walk
where there is no way,

on water,
filthy though it be,
unfree and
free.

Mourning Katrina is about devastation and
mourning, about the failure of humanity to act humanely,
about the politics of poverty and race, but it is also about
hope and healing. Like the CD "My Soul is Anchored"
that also came out of this project, this volume is about
the rainbow that comes after the storm and the revival of
spirit that comes out of the depths of tested faith. In the
final section that takes the name of the CD, the poems
reveal people who have absorbed the spirit of the blues
singers Ma Rainey and Bessie Smith by wrestling with
their suffering until they have transcended it. They draw
their power from long-standing traditions that cannot be
washed away by a flood or wiped out of the memory. Lena
Marie Ampadu, a NOLA native, opens this section with
New Orleans Street Memories:

> I REMEMBER THE STREETS OF NEW
> ORLEANS—MARDI GRAS DAY
> STREET PARADES WINDING THEIR
> WAY—THROUGH THE BROAD
> BOULEVARDS BRIMMING WITH THE
> BOLD COLORS OF PASSING FLOATS

Jan McGregor, another contributor, writes:

> Before the coup de grace of Katrina
> I remember you, Biloxi
> For June's blessing of the fleet
> Whose boats chugged out at dawn
> And returned in red sunset.

Only the lighthouse remains
Making me believe
In resurrection.

All of the poets in this section share one
characteristic: a willingness to see beyond their sorrow to
reinvent the spirit of the secondliners. Their witness makes
a joyful noise full of the sounds of "Laissez les bon Temps
rouler!" Though human suffering shaped the beginning of this
project, the result of it is a *morning* of hope and inspiration.
This project is dedicated to the survivors of Hurricane
Katrina, to the memory of all of those people who died as
a result of the storm, and to their families who are left to
mourn their loss.

Joanne V. Gabbin
James Madison University

And the Children Shall Lead Them

So Much Lost

Shame, shame, shame:
one day you have,
next day it's gone.
What does that feel like? I don't know.
I was one of the blessed ones.

Cars, clothes, and a house
are materials. Long as you have
your life, then you're in good shape.
God was looking out for many.

But when you look around,
you can't even tell that some have lost
so much.

Shola Adebamiji, 17
Baton Rouge, Louisiana

KATRINA

Why did it happen?
Why did it come?
Katrina was very bad!
It killed schools, trees, people too.
How can we help?
How can we stand this terrible disaster?
WE CAN GIVE!!

Caleb Amstutz, 8
Roanoke, Virginia

NOT the end

tear drops falling to make a natural disaster.
I've cried enough
enough to make children cry.
has this happened, Katrina? it has.
I want to do the best that I can to get things fixed.
but it is not the end.
it is a new beginning.
maybe the whole world will start over again.
maybe it will.
maybe I even will.
or it might all wash away
like the hurricane
                    it
               might

Celine Anderson, 8
Roanoke, Virginia

Katrina Brought Disaster

Katrina brought disaster
  She caused a lot of grief
    She showed the world destruction
    and pain beyond belief.
      Katrina split up families –
        She knocked their houses down.
        She took all their possessions
        and pulverized their town.
          Some women lost their husbands,
            some husbands lost their wives.
              Some people lost their neighbors,
              some children lost their lives.

Katrina's winds were massive.
  They took some heavy tolls.
    She may have caused catastrophe
    but deeply touched our souls.
      She brought us all together.
        United, here we stand.
          Our people heard a cry for help
          and lent a helping hand.
            We reassured the victims
            that help was on the way.
              We're doing all that we can do
              to brighten up your day.

Katrina may have knocked you down,
  but we will pick you up.
    She may have taken all your food,
      but we will fill your cup.
        You know you can rely on us.
          We'll be your shining sun.
            We are one nation under God.
            United we are one.

Latoya Anderson, 17
Baton Rouge, Louisiana

The Big Easy

People stuck on rooftops and in attics
Being filmed by national news fanatics
Looters raiding stores and shops
Cars being stolen by the cops
People getting a bad cough, or breaking out into hives
People losing everything, including their lives
Schools that are swamped with new children moving in
Family members desperately seeking kin
Others coming in from around the nation
Picking up the pieces, ending the frustration
Fixing the levees, stopping the water flow
Soon, we will hear the call of the Mardi Gras Mambo.
The Saints are moving to San Antonio?
Will the city be able to handle the blow?
There is only one thing in this city that is for sure
The Big Easy is not so easy anymore.

Blake Andrews, 14
Baton Rouge, Louisiana

Katrina . . . She Took Everything

She took my friends
She took my clothes
She took a lot of stuff and everyone knows.

She took my pictures
She destroyed my home
To rebuild my city will take long.

She took lives from people
She knocked down gates
The hurricane, Katrina, did not discriminate.

She made me cry
She made me hurt
Other hurricanes shall envy her.

She destroyed my relationships
She ruined my life
To go back home, one would have to think twice.

She was tough
She was bad
Katrina took everything I had.

She wouldn't stop
She wouldn't listen
She will never have competition.

She rearranged my future
She rearranged my goals
She made my whole life travel slow.
She drained my heart
She crushed my soul
Her horror stories will forever be told.

She drowned my city
The place I once knew
She changed the lives of others, too.

She was Katrina
She was a beast
She changed everything for me.

Tricia Bellot, 17
Baton Rouge, Louisiana

Destruction

Katrina is red, blue and gray
Flood and fire not kept at bay
Levees broke, gas lines broke
And Bay St. Louis washed away.

The marsh is gone, my house is gone
As rain came down all night long.
The south is changed for bad or worse
but we will be back ten times strong.

She changed our land but not our way
The food, the jazz and Mardi Gras parades.
We'll still be here dancing and having fun
She may have hurt but she has not won.

Glenn Buck, 16
Baton Rouge, Louisiana

Memories of a City

Memories of a city now forgotten to me
are lost forever to the August 29th tragedy,
for just as the flood waters rose
and those who were trapped lost hope,
I watched the culture die as the levees broke.
Tremé, the East, Gentilly, where the Indians roam,
were all lost in the place I used to call my home.
As the water recedes and the people flood back,
they see that their mansions and castles
have been reduced to caves and shacks.
Now the skyline has changed to fema blue,
and destruction and despair are all we see on the news.
Times seem gloomy for we know not what the future holds,
can we rebirth the birthplace of jazz?
Nobody knows.

Charles Burchell, 15
Baton Rouge, Louisiana

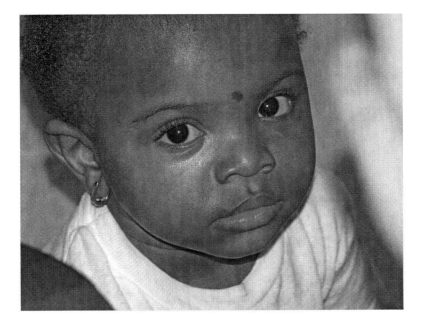

Cry for Katrina

Cry for those
who lost everything
Katrina came
and began destroying

Their houses are ruined
and they have no clothes
They were wearing the same thing
from their heads to their toes

Why did it take so long
to rescue them
Outside for four days
with no tub to wash in

So think about them
as you throw away meals
They have no food at all
you don't know how it feels

Don't waste your food
Instead, donate
You will still have food
But they have to wait!

Ericka Burke, 13
Baltimore, Maryland

Missing home

I haven't been there in so long
Riding through my neighborhood
To my home and it feels so good
That special place I've spent four years
That place I've shed so many tears
I wondered what it looks like now
But all in my head was this perfect house
As if we left it just the same
From the last time we came
My mind could think of nothing else
And so that memory I kept
My puppy walking up the stairs
The fusses, fights, wears, and tears
The good, the bad
All made me sad
As I walked through the door
And expected so much more
I started to cry as I saw the wooden frames
And the home feeling was cursed with pain
A cruel, horrible, vicious pain
A pain so difficult to obtain
And there was nothing I could do
But help clean up and start anew
I could not reverse the days
And push Katrina far away

If cleaning up my memories wasn't pain enough
A dump truck came and hauled it off as if it was just stuff
Some people call it material things
But I call it my memories
My sweet, sweet memories of how it used to be

My mind went back to the experience I had
The water rushing in so fast
Kicked us out of our first floor
When Katrina burst down the door
And I thought I was going to die
So in the attic I would lie
And wait for death to come to me
And death was all that I could see
Until my mom showed me the light
And I had hope with all my might
The water stopped flowing as fast
And God had saved us at last
But there we were stuck in that house
To wait this whole disaster out
The radio said about a week
But we barely had food to eat
And that night I could barely sleep
Because of the creatures and the heat
But after night came a sunny day
And I knew we would be okay

Helicopters passed overhead
But it was disappointment instead
Because they didn't stay that long
They looked down and carried on
Then these boats came passing by
Asking if we needed a ride
To the levee where we would stay
And burn up in the sun all day
They said that's all that they could do
And we knew it was probably true
Then we bid them good day
And when the day got longer
Somehow my hope got stronger
My family was all I had
And having them made me glad
Appreciation was in need
For all that they had given me
Their strengths alone made me strong
And gave me power to carry on
And cleaning up our house that day
Was reassurance we'd be okay
Because we were together then
And together now until the end
Because we're strong, whole, and brave
Unbreakable by even a hurricane
And as for me I'm living free, and loving life until I leave
And even then I'll be okay
Because I know I'll love that day.

Shawna Carey, 14
Baton Rouge, Louisiana

Blues Song for Katrina

Katrina, Katrina, why did you come?
Katrina, Katrina, what have you done?
You destroyed everything we've had
Now everyone in Baton Rouge is mad
Kids are bad and parents are sad
Everyone is using their last
You left us without a thing
Now we're begging and hugging
Realizing that New Orleans has come to an end
Now where do we begin
We have to start all over again
Katrina, you're just plain mean.
You left us with nothing, not even a string bean.

Brittany Dickson, 16
Baton Rouge, Louisiana

The Chaos

I was surprised everything was destroyed.
Hurricane Katrina was annoyed.
It looked like chaos.
Three states felt a loss.

Olivia Grubb, 9
Roanoke, Virginia

Water Line

A water line in a class room.
A line that separates circumstance.
Rich people above the line and poor people below.
Clean above the line and moldy below.

Rowan Gryder, 10
Roanoke, Virginia

Now

They had homes,
>   But now they're gone
They had families,
>   But now they're gone
No more kids,
>   'Cause now they're dead
No more schools,
>   'Cause no more tools
They had cars,
>   But now they're gone
They had fathers,
>   But now they're gone
No more brothers
>   Cause no more mothers
No more dogs
>   To give a hug
Now people are poor,
>   'Cause they don't have any more
No more money
>   People are just crying
>   It's a sad world,
>   Hurricane Katrina

Ashley Hammond, 12
Baltimore, Maryland

Cleaning off Katrina

In a defenseless house put against a destructive storm,
Four fragile walls hold strong,
But apparently not strong enough.
An elderly woman reappears to what she left:
Glistening china plates, now thick with grime,
Perfectly positioned tables, now upturned and disorderly,
Feathery bedspreads now hardened with grunge.
Mold and dirt climb the once decorative walls
like dense jungle vines,
Delicate designs become plastered underneath filth.
It is all heart wrenching,
But it is her life, nonetheless.
Making sure to preserve and protect her memories,
Scrubbing with yellow gloves,
Muddy balls, discovered to be
the old Christmas ornaments,
Soaking in plastic buckets,
Sludge drenched rags,
repaired into her gorgeous Easter dress,
Cleansing with chemicals,
Dirt clumps, uncovered to be
Grandpa's long forgotten coin collection.
Katrina covered the world with muck,
All we need to do now is wash it off.

Libby Ingram, 15
Baton Rouge, Louisiana

A Waterfall

Cry me a river and I'll give you a waterfall
filled with hope to cancel out all the pictures
painted by the unstoppable storm, which has
torn everyone away. Day-by-day we take
it one step at a time trying to figure out
which step we will take next. But, how can
we when our fathers and mothers are not
there to guide us, because they have been
lost in a world that no one knew would exist?
Cramped and overheated without space to
turn around, there is always an altercation
causing situations to get worse. What can
I do? What can I say? While everyone is
fleeing in separate ways, I am still stuck in
this one place. Will my home ever be the
same? Submerged and broken apart by
nature, and the terror of the loss kills
a part of me every day. But one day, it will
soon be over when that one drop will cancel
out all the hurt and loss. For I will cry me
a river and receive a waterfall filled
with hope.

Sherice King, 17
Baton Rouge, Louisiana

Head Up to Disaster

The scar of disaster
she left on our city.
Gone with the wind
and never to return
Leaving no trace
just helpless people
and broken spirits.
Life to live on, but not the same.
People point fingers but no one's the blame
We shall pick our head up
and go with faith
because God will lead us
the rest of the way.

Keaira Landry, 13
Baton Rouge, Louisiana

The Hurricane

Winds blow hard,
branches fly
Trees that are standing
Weep and cry
Quietness as the wind slows down
Rainfall as the fence turns brown
Easy breezy beautiful wind blows
Trees fall instead of grow.
Rain goes with wind
Squirrels run as if there's a person within
Umbrellas fly in the opposite direction
Kids cry for they cannot fulfill their TV obsession
Sun shines to tease Ms. Rita
just showing that God can beat her.
Disasters that never happened before
Rita comes and destroys the outdoors.
Louisiana stands up and says, "No more!"
"She will not destroy us because she's living in Category 4!"
We shall just clean up the mess and live on
because the end of hurricane season won't be long.

Keaira Landry, 13
Baton Rouge, Louisiana

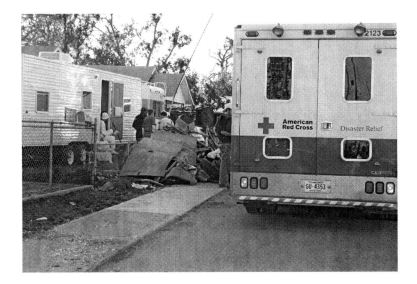

Death Came after a Holy Day

Death came after a holy day
She even came in a disastrous way
Safety and insurance were gone
Tears of mourning and sorrow
With no food or money to borrow
Families became lost and unfound
I personally started to feel bound
Saved but still scared from the feeling of exile
People treated us as if we were wild
With daylight around us but darkness among us
The weight of people's attitude felt like a ton
I still feel as though I need to run.

Craig Lawson, 17
Baton Rouge, Louisiana

Untitled

Hush! Now look back at Katrina. Look at all the pain
and suffering people
went through just to stay
alive, taking care of
their kids, cousins, and
themselves at the same time.
Huh! Now look at America
people acting like they
really care.
People acting like they
can't give up a few dollars
to help the homeless, the
loneliness.
Now look at Bush -- come a
week later after hundreds die,
he could have tried to
help the kids survive and
stay alive.
They left a group of people
to die, hot and lonely in an
elderly home.
People crying, flying, trying
to save their friends and
family members.
Having flashbacks on memories.
Ain't that a shame, it ain't a
game.
But it's all okay -- maybe
God said, "All the people who
died, it was their day."

Mishonia Lee, 12
Baltimore, Maryland

Ready or Not

A new day with the sun so bright
Good morning New Orleans, what a wonderful night!
Open my eyes to start a new day,
Turn on the news -- what will the weather say?
Ready or not, I can't believe
Hurricane Katrina and everyone must leave.
Is this real or just another bluff?
I think they're joking so I'll leave all my stuff,
Just take a few clothes; we will be back.
By lunch time Katrina will fall off track.
As we load the car I take a look at my special things
I treasure most,
Going down the road, running from the coast.
We had a big family and everyone should have come...
but when we hit the highway each car became one.
Cousin Stacy off to Atlanta,
Brother Tave to Northern Louisiana,
Cousin Adam in Tennessee,
and we are in Florida – how can this be?
How could Katrina break up our family?
The highway is busy, no rooms available to stay.
We can't sleep in the car. We have to turn, but which way?
We found a hotel and the news is on.
Katrina came through and New Orleans is gone.
What about the bluff?
Oh, God, this is real.
No one knows the pain I feel.
I should have packed my dance awards,
my honor trophies and writing rewards.
I wanted to take my new doll and bike,
my new doll house and cheerleading sack.
Now I can't go back.

What happened to my friend next door?
She said she would ride out the storm.
Her house is flooded and no one's home.
I hope she made it to the Superdome.
As I try to call her, I can't get through.
I want to say, Girl, I miss you.
Ready or not, it's time for another part
Goodbye Osborne Elementary. It's a new start.
As I walk up the stairs I take a deep breath.
I smile at my sister as she says, No sweat.
I feel at home as everyone smiles at me.
I hear a voice, *Welcome to Highland Elementary.*
I think I can manage. Everything is cool.
A new home, new friends, and an awesome school.

Kaylin LeVaseur, 10
Baton Rouge, Louisiana

Katrina

She came through like a wild animal,
destroying everything in her path,
the damage she made was ample,
Taking no mercy.
A whole city is gone.
It will be rebuilt with love.
Whoever said New Orleans is done
is wrong.

Lance Mathis, 17
Baton Rouge, Louisiana

Where I Live

Where I live is now
where I used to live.
The bed I sleep in is now
the bed I slept in.
The white tile floor I walk on is now
the horror-stained tile
never to be walked on again.
A life once treasured has gone.

Tracy Nguyen, 16
Baton Rouge, Louisiana

The Flood

Water rises
The foundation floods with
tears of a family
water rises
Seats that sat in warmth
sit no longer
water rises
Memories in pictures
melt away
water rises
My eyes are
    flooded
water rises.

Michael San Miguel, 15
Baton Rouge, Louisiana

Shout Outs to the Hurting

Devastations and tragedies come and go
And there are so many hurts and woes
Wars and deaths, they break your heart
You do not know when or where they will start
Hurricane Katrina tore up New Orleans
Everything will be alright soon – don't worry
My heart goes out to those of you who lost loved ones
Many of you have lost daughters and sons
To wars and to natural disaster
It seems that your whole life has been shattered

But I am here to tell you everything will be alright
Just ride it out and hold on tight
For I am telling you I see the end in sight
So just sit back, relax, and enjoy the flight.

I know everyone is not perfect but
You should not go through life with your eyes shut.
It is like limping through life without a crutch.
You would be tripping over things and getting out.
This is why it is not right to sin
Because you never know when your life could end.
I see everyone I know trying to fit in
That is why most of them are in the pen.
People out there selling drugs
They out there trying to be thugs.
But through all that they look for love
But find nothing, so they push and shove
But sometimes all they need is a big ol' hug
And the comfort from the creator above

Even though you have been hurt and broken
Jesus Christ is your best token.
He is the only one that can save you.
He is the only one whose love is true.
He helps you through and through.
He helps you when you are down and blue.
So let him come and take his place
Talk to him while you sleep and are awake.
Give the Lord your soul to take
Let him hold you for his love is not fake.

Arthur Scott, 17
Baton Rouge, Louisiana

Katrina, Katrina, Katrina

Katrina, Katrina, Katrina
What have you done
You tore down houses
People can't even see the sun
Katrina, Katrina, Katrina
People laying around
Kids are lost
Everyone getting a different kind of disease.

Katrina, Katrina, Katrina
The water is past my stomach
No stores are open
Kids can't go to school
Adults can't go to work.

Katrina, Katrina, Katrina
People have no shelter, no clothes
No tissue, no food
Katrina, Katrina, Katrina
I can't believe what you have done.
Katrina, Katrina, Katrina
Look what you have done
Katrina, Katrina, Katrina

Abi Solomon, 11
Baltimore, Maryland

Hurricane Katrina

Hurricane Katrina, so sad and bad.
It makes it hard to find words for such a drag.
Why do things like this happen? I ask.
For the results of such terrible things are rash.
Why do all those people share such a fate?
I don't know, but when I do find out,
I just hope it isn't too late.

Audrey Stephenson, 9
Roanoke, Virginia

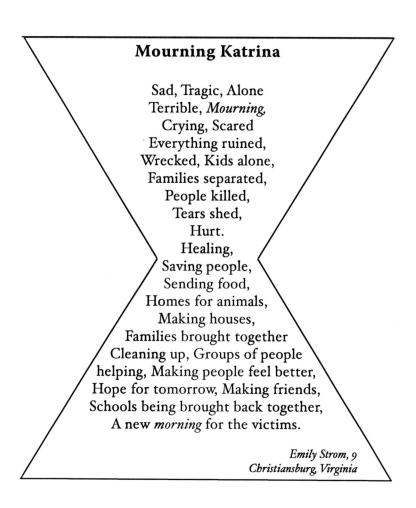

Mourning Katrina

Sad, Tragic, Alone
Terrible, *Mourning,*
Crying, Scared
Everything ruined,
Wrecked, Kids alone,
Families separated,
People killed,
Tears shed,
Hurt.
Healing,
Saving people,
Sending food,
Homes for animals,
Making houses,
Families brought together
Cleaning up, Groups of people
helping, Making people feel better,
Hope for tomorrow, Making friends,
Schools being brought back together,
A new *morning* for the victims.

Emily Strom, 9
Christiansburg, Virginia

Sympathy

You look at the mess
in your white velvet dress.
You think to look away
but you run to the sea bay.
A tear rolls down your cheek.

Eric Sutton, 10
Montvale, Virginia

Katrina
awake night

Wind blowing,
I immerse in somber street, alone.
Heavy soul,
cohered by actuality in a long time,
bring me into that horrible night. . . . . .

Katrina, wake sleeping people.
The once scene is changed hugely.
Losing the direction,
I hover in the familiar street,
try to survive in the dark alarmedly,
however, I can't find exit.

The whole city
was shrouded by stifling sorrow,
lost its sheen and spirit,
people are summoning in the darkness.

Hopeful father, scorched in heart,
break one after another actual dreams
into foam . . . . . .
Tears blur eyes.

The heart, desired hanker
encourage the left zest
burn the withered, waiting soul
until extinguishing.
Still don't know where to go

Unfortunately!
Remaining sick at heart
      and drifting soul
To drift for waiting people

Jue Wang, 16
Baton Rouge, Louisiana

Surprise

Katrina came as a surprise
Never had I experienced something so bizarre
In the North this is unheard of
In the South it's a part of life
But how can one get accustomed to something
that causes so much strife?
A disaster underestimated
The aftermath? Never exaggerated
Tons of water swamped masses of land
It's a blessing so many offered a helping hand
Katrina's effect couldn't be predicted
But I do believe that it was predestined
Leaving destruction in her path
We can't dwell on the aftermath
It is time to start out fresh
And put the hands of man to the test.

Andrea Wilkins, 17
Tougaloo, Mississippi

Oh, Katrina

Katrina, Oh Katrina, you blew my home away
All because of you, in my home town I couldn't stay
Oh I hate you Katrina, you forever changed my life
I will always blame you for putting me through
this pain and strife
Maybe you were trying to clean New Orleans
from all the evil and sin
but that's no excuse for dispersing my friends
that I might never see again

Jeron Williams, 15
Baton Rouge, Louisiana

I Just Don't Know

I just don't know why
I didn't bring my rabbit with me
When I heard Hurricane Katrina was coming
I'm sorry for leaving him behind
I can imagine how it felt when he was drowning
All that water flowing in his mouth
For hours
No way to get out
No food to eat.

Chantell Williams, 12
Baton Rouge, Louisiana

History in the Water

We Can't Step into the Same River Twice

My daughter's worried, says she heard that the
Live Oaks in City Park can't breathe underwater,
and the ducks who bit her small hands full of bread,
"Who will feed them?".
She imagines the Aquarium fish swimming away
quick silver flashes like our pond's minnows, only freer.
The elephants large as memory will wade out
like ships from the zoo, maybe rescue smaller animals.
But a poem's
not a life line, and the poet, not a boat.

These places burning,
flooding at the same time; these buildings
where I've said to my daughter, "This is where you were
born, and your father and his father.
Your great grandparents
were married at St. Louis Cathedral.
Grandma Cherry
used to say that the gardenias in New Orleans
bloomed so much that the bees flew drunkenly
into her kitchen windows all afternoon.
And here,
here's where your father and I met.
Because this is there, we are here."
But we aren't here anymore,
and we haven't traveled lightly on purpose.
Nobody predicts when it will stop,
and no one when anything will begin again.
My friend's 5 year old daughter kneels,
thanks God "for our house that has a tree on it."
She'll start kindergarten elsewhere
in borrowed plaid uniforms.
Their parrot
that was rescued is not simply renamed Lucky.
From a shelter
outside Houston, a dozen of who we call ours finally call us.
On TV the city's sounds are hundreds of dogs calling for
someone across this filthy slow moving water. A man and
a woman paddle an air mattress with brooms to anyplace
else, and the anchor says again, "The city is a bowl. The
city is a bowl." until I too am too full.

Malaika King Albrecht
Pine Hurst, North Carolina

reflections

1. a question from my wandering people

where are you Moses?
our wilderness is flooding.
your Bush doesn't care.

2. breaking commandments

during exodus,
I dream of burning a Bush
whose name is Pharoah.

3. a pastor's lamentations
   (or a wake up call for Black folks
   who voted republican in 2004)

"if you did not know
you were Black before this week
you should know by now."

4. moaning the blues while jazz is
drowning

Satchmo is silent
amidst wails from the dead who
cry, "God is not pleased."

tori omega arthur
Alexandria, Virginia

Storm Surge

It was always friendly to us,
as long as I can remember.
We used to sit near it, and
sometimes, when momma
wasn't looking, we'd dip our
toes into it.

Never even showed us a dark eye.

We'd tip our hats to it, and it
returned the gesture by bathing
our faces in it from the razor-like
beams from the summer sun.

Then, it came, stood up as tall as
an oak, spreading its cowl like an
angry, spitting cobra.

It came howling, with a broad chest,
bloody eyes. It came, taller now,
casting a shadow on all the neighborhood.
(funny how it did that; we always looked down
at it, below our knees).

But, it came, bullied by foreign waters, and whistling
wind much taller than it, much taller than *our* knees.
Noble is it till the end; it apologized for
the stranger's rude manners, and praised.

Bruce Baker
Henderson, Nevada

The Belly of the Beast

I could not make out the numbers
Etched in its skin as it hovered above,
Wings eliciting a calm heartbeat.

The wings spiraled about, disturbing
The aging shingles, swollen with rain.
And somehow I knew the world below

Had rested their case; I would now be
Relegated to the hovering beast, and
Ushered off to the blue night sky.

Bruce Baker
Henderson, Nevada

Last Journal Entry

Mental pictures of this devastation
Could never be erased.
As I stand and pace the floor,
Like Shakespeare I'm searching for my lost Lenore.
See, she's been missing for four days and four nights,
And together we have four beautiful kids with four bikes.
All that was taken from me within one night,
The night Hurricane Katrina took flight.
She took my house, my kids and my wife,
And without them I have no reason to fight for life.
But it's my fault, I thought if we stayed the storm
wouldn't take form,
I was misinformed.
In one night I lost my house and my wife,
And not to mention our four beautiful kids with
Four bikes.
After seeing this devastation what's my purpose in life?
I have no wife, no kids to love, and no home to
Go back to, so who am I now?
How do I recover from death?
I take a deep breath,
And realize that if I want to regain my life
I must join my kids and my wife,
In the afterlife.

Derrick Calvert
Vicksburg, Mississippi

Count With Me

Every now and then I have to remind my little brother to
count with me
He is only ten and yet he can carry the weight of the world
He is only ten and yet he carries the weight of the world
He is indeed my protector, my home and my strength
But every now and then I have to remind my little brother
to count with me
Before he begins to fantasize over guns and drugs
Before he lets his mind become raped by girls and thugs
I say come here my little brother and
count with me
Before he watches 50 and Yayo make the hood alright
with Britney Spears jingles
I'll say count with me

And sometimes his heart is heavy,
he misses his older brother 'cause
It is hard to hear him count through 10-inch glass
put up by the warden
Hard to hear his voice tremble over his lips
When he writes his numbers in a letter
And he only sees his big brother write those numbers
about once a month
Because his brother has no job, no income, no education
And in jail rent is a dollar a day
When he gets sad, upset or afraid
He comes to me and I hear him say,
Daisha come count with me
When teachers say he can't keep up in a class of 20 students
And move him into a class of 35
He says count with me

In his later years, when he sees his friends up
against a wall with flashlights in their eyes
Reads about classmates found under staircases
Old girlfriends dumped in alleys or dumped by men
who saw their love begin to take life
 and shape inside of their bellies,
he says count with me
He will say count with him as tears roll down my face
as I pack a bag for him
I won't see him for awhile, I am sending him away
Because I won't let my brother die in a war
they say is being fought for a cause that don't
mean shit to us

Bullets will not fly past his head,
scrap metal will not pierce his body
Soldiers will not knock on my door with their
heads hung low and their news of death
Offering me a flag as the last memory of my brother
I don't want that flag
And he doesn't know that flag
So he leaves and they will not get him
And he calls me all the time
He knows me well
He knew to call me after Katrina hit
Knew I was a big mess
Calm down Daisha, he would say, and count with me
1 no other, 2 balance, 3 trinity
When I sat and watched mothers hold dying babies
And young children rock the old before
 they passed out into an eternal dream
Tears rolled down my face and my stomach tightened
And my brother would say
Count with me

'Cause honestly it would only take one person
to make one big difference
One bottle of water for one husband
to live to see his one wife
One pill to ease the pain that this storm has made
One shot for one mother to wake up
to see her six kids the next day

'Cause when the cameras zoomed in on bodies
That were ignored by the government
And unrecognizable by the family,
He said count with me
One call that would allow 400 doctors to save
one thousand eyes from crying their last tear at night
One eye to see what really is going on here
One law that really cares about the supplies
truly getting down there

'Cause on the third day after citizens lose all
that 11 thousand dollars a year could buy them
The government sends troops to stop the looting,
count with me
Soldiers are there with guns and weapons and water and
food to make sure they have strength to use
those guns and weapons
And yet thousands are dying without water,
food, and medicine,
count with me

And it would only take one van to take back one family so
they won't have to be found dead in the street

One just one
It takes one person to walk away before
they continue to be forgotten
One person to stop crying so the government can start
lying about who truly destroyed the levees
One person to forget that someone was drowning
as she was counting the calories that one warm morning

But there was no urgency, there was no care
People have died and people continue to die for
this government's lack of responsibility
Yet it will only take one person to open her home
to one child that just woke up an orphan
One heart that DOES instead of talking about
what he wishes he could do
One just One
and that could just be you

But too many of us wait until tomorrow
And too many of us wait for someone else
to take charge
So too many of them were left
to make asphalt their burial grounds
And still too many of us don't care

So three days passed and they waited
Three days passed and they were hungry
Three days passed before we started moving
And one by one
Two by two
And three by three
They   Died
Four   WHAT?

So, no they won't replace my brother with a flag
'Cause at the Superdome an old lady wrapped
the flag around her shoulders to help keep warm
And right about now that's all it's good for
So keep your flag.

Ladaisha Ballard
Joy Petway
Harrisonburg, Virginia

Sitting Ducks at the Superdome

One day in America the dirty secrets were revealed
Hurricane Katrina, Neglect and the Levee broke
New Orleans August 2005
God bless America

African Americans herded into a Superdome,
Lying, dying in darkness waiting to be rescued,
Waiting for the descendants who captured
their ancestors into slavery,
Forcing them in shackles ashore
on the waters to the Americas,
Cramped tight on ships where many died
of lack of food and water.
Waiting they sit in the Superdome,
Cramped tight dying of lack of food and water.
Surrounded by the dirty sewer swamp waters
of New Orleans.

Without electricity, air conditioning broken,
no one in authority "It is a free for all."
Backup toilets and no running water,
The stench forces the soldiers to wear masks,
Afraid to enter the washrooms
that stink of human waste and thugs
People resort to defecating in the open area
of this here Superdome.
Outside water knee deep,
corpse floats and disease abounds,
Dehydrated in sweltering heat they wait,
Sitting ducks herded into a hell hole
controlled by men in army fatigues and guns,
Children cry, old people die, thugs shoot
Women exhausted holding their babies
Men wandering, yelling,
futile attempts whose fruits bear nothing,
having lost their instincts to protect and to survive.
Sitting ducks hold up in America.
Where were the men when Tinisha got raped?
Where were the men when Cathy
jumped and broke her ankles to escape
a car jacking and attempted rape?
Where were the men?
Sitting ducks hold up in the Superdome
Lost all ability to be leaders,
lost all ability to protect women and children?
Sitting, waiting, sighing, cursing
Where were the men?

People scramble for food, water and diapers
from closed stores,
The looters raid the stores for guns and CDs,
Miscued priorities, thugs shooting and raping,
 you can't shoot water.
Chaos and still they wait 4 days before
the first rescue convoy of trucks
arrive with food, water and guns.
"Point your guns down" the soldiers are ordered

The GUN only thing they know.
The GUNS to take control.
The plight, trauma and sadness have turned to anger,
Race and class are uttered off the lips of many,
Would it take so long to rescue
Middle Class White America?

This lack of response is so blatant, bold -faced and racist
No love, No compassion,
The dirty secrets of America revealed. We all see
the poverty in their sunken eyes, swollen bellies.
Ill clad clothing on the sun burnt backs
of the black people
Where are the Indians, the Native Americans?
What happened to them?
Old black man with a cane limps with a flour sack,
as he makes his way to an airplane.
2005 or is he a sharecropper in 1905 ?
A slave visiting us through a time machine?

Dead woman sits in a wheel chair
with a blanket on her face,
 Someone's mother, a grandmother,
Teenager has a diabetic coma,
" I don't want to die like this."
Families torn apart, values and dignity torn asunder.
Woman cries with her dead husband at her side,
wrapped in a shroud he survived the hurricane.
Died from lack of medical attention.
Middle age black man wails for his dead wife
holding his two young sons,
"she gone" ... he retells the journalist shooting the image,
his wife letting go of his hand,
 his home splitting in two her last words... .
" you can't hold me, take care of the kids and grand kids"
Hurricane Katrina, floods caused from neglect
broke the levee and revealed to the world
the underbelly of American society.
The Emperor's naked, the under Bush speaks the truth.
"that part of the world"
Isn't New Orleans a part of America?
while Laura Lee speaks of how well
the White people in La la land
have managed to organize and stem the tide of chaos.
The hidden racist message plain to see...

A country vulnerable to natural and human disasters
that many with warped minds
are now fine tuning their plans on how to exploit
this new found knowledge,
as they work in the middle of the night
to bring America to its knees.

Sitting ducks are my brothers and sisters.
Sitting ducks are all of us.
We have lost our instincts to survive in the wild.
A wake up call to plan and prepare
for whatever dreams and nightmares may come.
Roof tops, attics and superdomes can't be our answers.
Sitting ducks in the Americas.

Claire Carew
Toronto, Canada

Katrina Blues

I.
I've come to remind them
to place this magnified eye
against the sophistry they cover
with a scrim of patriotism & piety

I've come to show them
what undone freedom looks like
to belch up their underbelly in a
shock of wind & water

I've come to remind them
that they have not created
the earth they seek to destroy
nor the people they chain to race & class

They will say my name in terror
rue my existence
rebuilding both their lives
& their lies.

II.
"We're burning & we're looting tonight" Bob Marley

Niggas loot, white folks find
this is the science, scripture
spewed from the frothy mouths
of reporters, who ignored dying
grandmothers to give us this scoop:
the unwashed masses, their poor asses
were stealing, pads & pampers, bread
& water & lawd no, TVs too.

Niggas loot, white folks find
& white folks found it hard to
believe that black folks would not
die solemn deaths, that we would
not dehydrate with dignity while
our govt. watched our suffering
with muted concern or excited amusement

Niggas loot, white folks find,
we find this easier to understand
than how W got elected twice or
how 20 thousand people can be
forgotten & warnings ignored

Niggas loot, white folks find
& we find ourselves here again
the Sisyphus of our reality
a historic requirement to defy
immoral laws that protect water-logged
DVDs more than water-logged elders

So we're looting tonight
refusing to surrender to the
devastation of wind, water,
or white supremacy.

III.
"We're the survivors, the black survivors" Bob Marley

we know about the fury of wind,
of water dark with disease & malice
we know the stark terror that says
"save them right after you save the livestock"

we have lived in black bottom settlements
learned to love each other next to levees
constructed with our labor cheapened by
Jim Crow threats.

in this maelstrom we make music
find nourishment in heavenly sins
as we await the creators' judgment,
a promise to make us equal in eternity.

Kenneth Carroll
Washington, District of Columbia

No Ark

Water, water everywhere, and not a drop to drink.
-Samuel Taylor Coleridge

Day 1
I thought she would be like the others.
Come, then go. No fuss. No big deal.
I propped myself and my stuff
against the doors and windows.
All cracks and seams sealed.
Just in case she decided to
hang around for a while. And she did. Like a
wild child, letting her would be hair down.
Brought 30 foot waves, with no smile or
hello. Just, hell you know.
Rain so heavy, so sharp, drops shattered
leaving marquise and emerald cuts as they
landed on skin, in eyes. I could not see
her approaching, but heard a howling
outside. I could not comprehend how bad;
nor calculate, or do the math,
that five more days would pass.

Day 2
What woke me was something running.
Like the faucet was left on. Something
leaking, a valve open, but I
was still sleeping and alone. Floating weightless
into consciousness, a breeze tip-toed
across my nose, opened my eyes.
It felt like I was drowning. Previously,
God said, *Let there be...* but the whole city
was now without light. Thanked Him
for the sun, the moon and the stars. But
they too seemed to be out of order. As if
the universe did not have a back-up generator.

We had lost our power.

Day 3
Sink or swim. I remember taking lessons
at the public pool donated to the YMCA in
Jackson Square when I was a boy. The date
escapes me, because now I was wading
and escaping was just what I was trying to do.
After 8 hours I finally made it to the roof. Felt like
I had just worked the day shift as I sifted and
punched through. But what I saw when I
reached the night air, the levees were gone, no
longer there, *water, water everywhere.*
There was no where to go. And if so, then where to.

Day 4
I was never good at cooking. But, I was baking
my ass off on the roof top. I was convinced that
someone would smell the sizzling of my now
burnt, sun-kissed skin. Maybe they would think
it was southern fried chicken and come running.
I mean, floating by to save me.
All those thoughts had now made
me hungry. But more than that, I was thirsty.
All of this water, and there was none to drink.
I begin to think. Others must be this way
as well. Maybe I should yell. As I begin to get
louder and louder, it became harder and harder
to breathe, I was dehydrating. I thought if I jumped
in the water that may assist me in reviving. As I
stepped to the edge, I hedged, saw bubbling
bodies fermenting--contaminating.
Like a raisin in the sun, I was drying.

Day 5
I had been praying all along, today I tried to
add songs. Hymns or gospel tunes. But, all I could
recall was *He's Got The Whole World In His Hands.*
I sure hoped that was true, not just an exercise
I learned in Vacation Bible School.

In high school I took wood shop. I wanted to
become a carpenter like my elder brother. I admired
him for his dedication, skill and attention
to detail. He was the Master of woodwork.
A boat would sure come in handy right now.

Day 6
The days were long, but the nights even longer. Cold
like deep south night winters. And with the water
surrounding it was more chilling, I thought surely
this was going to kill me. I wanted to be safe, and
dry, and clean. Wanted to feel the steam from the hot
bath that I had last. Instead, I saw it rising from the
Bayou each morning. Lake Pontchartrain had become
the ocean and the sea. The mouth of the Gulf of Mexico
was now right next to me. And it was wide. Lost track of
time. Instead I counted waves. 144. One each hour,
every hour for how I spent my days. This
kept me focused to some degree. That perhaps
with all my praying and crying, my faith would guide
someone to me. At my faintest moment,
I still believed. With my last breath I cried out to the
heavens one more time *God please save me.*

Day 7

.

Deborah D. Grison
Union City, New Jersey

Business as Usual

today

so many things to pray for
so many things to do
right now
the hardest is
fighting back tears
accepting reality of blackness
it's not a color
            not a class
not a location

it's when your leaders
forget to care
or at least act like they do to win
popular approval
like the prayer congress recited September 12
on national television
slapping the faces of their non-Christian citizens
jumping on the four fathers' graves
combining church and state
they were too late
with each day
the toll rose
as families worried,
wondered if their
loves would come home

and today

so many things to come to terms with
so many things to hold in
right now
the most important action is
saving my people
the ones forgotten
the ones
still treading waters of former bayous
heavy with humidity
and waterlogged jambalaya recipes
and mildewing living room furniture
and rusting saxophones
and spilled cups of Bourbon and Hurricane
inebriating lifeless bodies
floating
like chicory grains on water
brewing a hot mug of
infection
disease
and
tears

and like then
the toll rises
but not like then
the toll didn't have to be so damn high!

they were too late!
5 days is too long
and it doesn't take that long to respond
...when you care
don't condemn Kanye
for calling the devil a devil

and today

I sit tired
from incessant praying
that I can do my part,
the part our leaders forgot to do

be not me a
pillar of salt

I never turned my back to begin with
running away
in 2005
is not an option
for my people
the world got to see firsthand
how unequal
protocol is when you're
in a darker shade of skin
none of us can avoid mother nature's temper tantrums
especially when we keep pissing her off
mistreating the earth is so unwise
cause when she lets off steam
the waters rise

they   let   our   families   die

this is not the first time
our humanity has been ignored
our families separated and scattered
extending the meaning of 'diaspora'

and today

so many things to gather
so much strength to amass
until they've all arrived
one
bus
at
a
time

get on the bus

leave no children behind
leave no mothers or brothers
behind either

they've turned to pillars of salt
'cause they turned their backs
and were forced to face their ineptness
after all
resign or get impeached
it's called for this time.

Melanie Michelle Henderson
Washington, District of Columbia

The Last Door

In Goreé
The Last Door
an aperture, a hole
a doorway cut in stone,
in time

one side African
the next unfree

slave

American apartheid
one sign White
the other   unfree

Colored

All our days colored
with bitter erasure
of our names

the half-erased
discolorings of our competence,
our selves

the second seat
or the last

The Last Door, out of fetid, dank darkness
out of the flood

seeping under
into our shabby shoes

until we walk
a ragged step
like people in shackles

but walk
where there is no way,

on water,
filthy though it be,

unfree and
free.

Angela Jackson
Chicago, Illinois

Somebody Prayed for Me

Somebody had to have prayed for me because
I denied Katrina would ever be
tearing down power lines making me think back in time
of Emmett Till's face . . . as Katrina began
causing death to the Gulf Coast like foreign weapons of
mass destruction.

Somebody had to have prayed for me because

I had been partying the night before
age 19 thinking back once more
about life so far in New Orleans
Saving my last dance for next week's party
not noticing Katrina would displace me
away from home without food, shelter, or clothes
This could not be a part of my life.
To wake up on the road fleeing from a storm
I watch babies moan
Traffic crowd New Orleans interstates
I witnessed a man's face shattered in glass
from his car hitting the back of an 18 wheeler
so, I know someone had to have prayed for my soul.

Fleeing from Katrina
made me motherless
            fatherless
            without siblings

If you ever want to know how it feels to be displaced,
come find me,
and I'll tell my story of going without.

            For, I was once a New Orleans resident
            a black college student making use of the
            power of independence.

Now, I am labeled a refugee
Regardless of my journey through seven or more states;
I am still labeled by an ee.
Yet, somebody must have prayed for me.
I am alive.

Ciara Jeffery
Washington, District of Columbia

She Changed Me

Katrina changed me, brought me away
in time, battered with segregation and . . .
poor determination.
Where Jim Crow's laws stay inside my mind
like numbers (including 911).
Katrina put the spotlight on
African Americans in the media.
Blacks are: poor
            helpless
            dependent
            illiterate

Stereotypes that share no sympathy for any
human being of this nation.

So what:
if I am black with no huge home,
I am no Hilton or Bush,
I am a taxpayer just like any other citizen,
I am no refugee,
I am an American,
I am no criminal.
My people are not criminals
because in times of disaster,
waiting on the government for food,
clothing, and water is like waiting for the snow
to appear in New Orleans.

New Orleans was my loving city.
A city where bread winners came from the ghetto.
A city with its own language
and diaspora of mixed origins.
New Orleans was a place of sacrifice
Survival
Grandma's wise tales
Land of Voodoo
Seafood
Mardi Gras
and Fiestas.

Katrina changed me.
I am displaced from my city.

Ciara Jeffery
Washington, District of Columbia

Mourning Katrina

She came so fast
didn't know her trademark would last
she has made history
yet her troubled waters proved a mystery
our nation lies in misery
while faces laugh and grin with envy
the Gulf Coast cherish memories that are
left behind
time after time after . . . time
Still no call from them
My loved ones, not all could swim
drive cars
even speak the word, "Help"
They were blinded by late evacuation notices
lost faith and turned around
Now today they reign underground or
up in the mist of the clouds.
They reign amongst strangers
with invisible faces.

And today they themselves are now,
invisible.

Ciara Jeffery
Washington, District of Columbia

Katrina's Survivor

Don't call me refugee
The blasphemy, casualties
Anorexia stands a part of me
Broken lungs and ribs of my people
blacken like watermelon seeds

Ciara Jeffery
Washington, District of Columbia

Casualties

Casualties crowd toxic neighborhoods
Rats camouflage the floors of the Convention
  Center and Superdome.
  Darkness cause death along with
    long cries of healing
    shattered glass
      roof leaks of hot air

Children die waiting for a dumpster to load food
Elderly die from waiting on medication
Young children learn at an early age
  that FEMA's no show means steal
  and go.
Stillborn babies are sent to heaven
  humming FEMA.
  Gasoline is too high
  Order and equality start to question faith

It was the Gulf Coast calling amazing
grace.

And no one answered, but God
The Gulf Coast counted on Homeland Security
  and Bush.

Yet, administering to souls is too much.
So, many on their death beds lie waiting
  for assistance,
Still many wait for food and water
And still blacks, Caucasians, Latinos, and
all races including the others lie
                              dead
                              smashed
                              curled like snails
                    waiting the account of the death
                    toll in heaven.
          Singing the words from Martin Luther King, Jr.,
          "Free at last! Free at last! Thank God
          Almighty we're free at last!"
Hopefully, they are free in heaven.

Ciara Jeffery
Washington, District of Columbia

Hurricane Haiku

I.
Mother, father, son
Wind, rain, slain, agony
Morning, refugee now

II.

Bomb, atomic bomb
Death, destruction, poverty
Invincible, I think not

III.

Tears fall from my eyes
The sounds of babies' cries, death
It hurts my soul, why

IV.

Yesterday, Darfur
Today, hoy, New Orleans
Apocalypses

Julian Johnson
Chicago, Illinois

TEARS

For my brother, I cry
For my sister, I cry
From my people, I weep

Julian Johnson
Chicago, Illinois

She Was

Down the street she walks
She defines grace
Can't you see it?
It's the way she moves, those eyes that
sooth
Grace

Salt of the earth, that's what she was
Or at least that's what she *was*

New Orleans

Julian Johnson.
Chicago, Illinois

Aerial

There is an aging black woman in New Orleans,
seated in her wheelchair on the roof
of her home, a house with slanted eaves.

She waves her hands and no one responds. Waters
flow like rapids on either side of her unhinged security
door. Technology: we watch. My son asks, how

did that woman get there, and I talk to him
about what a woman will do to feel safe: climb
and cut, heave and hoist. But the wheelchair,

he says, how did she get on her roof
in that wheelchair with no other people
around her. Humanity: we ache. It is more

than a problem of logic— nothing adds up
to an aging black woman in a wheelchair on a roof,
exclusive between commercials on the six o'clock news.

Jacqueline Jones LaMon
New York City, New York

Cut Trina?

Simple me, I asked why
When they sliced-up the Continental pie
We got crumbs or none?

European answered:
Indians are not human.

EuroMerican chimed in:
Africans ain't men.

Redneck responded:
Nigger, you Know!

Conservative said:
Poor Colored Boys...SO.

Liberal Bleated:
Give Negroes a place in line,
After mine.

Progressive Pontificated:
African Americans are SO unsophisticated.

Radical Ruminated:
Black Fodder.

The Katrina washed-out,
My remaining doubt:
Players have new names,
Same roles, old games.

K.L.—Ol' Head Talkin'

Kinard Lang
Philadelphia, Pennsylvania

The Only World I've Ever Known

the river's vapors hover like a shade,
sheltering the banks and the water from the flames
Dante. The Inferno. Canto XV.

The only world I've ever known, for good
or ill, lies within a bowl of mountains.
Even when the waters rise and the French Broad
overflows, it does not reach my door.

Now I watch the venerable city, held
in a bowl between lake and sea, where Percy
and Faulkner launched bright words
and old men drew the blues up from their grief
in a wooden hall called preservation,
the city of dance and dark where the dead
lurk above the ground and absinthe flows
from wormwood into gall, where sex and food
and even Elysium do not spell paradise—now I watch
as the city drowns.

Displaced, displaced and nameless,
they plead from rooftops
above the liquid streets,
apocalypse an understatement.

my soul is anchored:
poems from the
mourning Katrina
national writing project

furious flower
poetry center
JAMES MADISON UNIVERSITY.

JAMES MADISON
UNIVERSITY.

FURIOUS FLOWER POETRY CENTER

MSC 3802
Harrisonburg, VA 22807

"... the rainbow that comes after the storm and the revival of spirit that comes out of the depths of tested faith."

My soul is anchored: poems from the mourning Katrina national writing project, a CD of spoken word and gospel music, is available at www.jmu.edu/furiousflower. Or send a check payable to JMU Furious Flower Poetry Center for $12.95 plus $2 for shipping and handling to:

Furious Flower Poetry Center
James Madison University
MSC 3802
Harrisonburg, VA 22807

For further information,
please call (540) 568-6310.

Safe in the world I've always known,
I welcome people to the wedding
of our son. We dance and laugh
as if the world were not coming to an end
in one old city, as if chance
had not run out with all its chips and cards,
drowning its sorrows with the green fairy,
no more parades with masks
and coins or white umbrellas, the blues
always was good music to die by.

Fire and water fill my mind
and one chiseled face,
a young black woman dying, her rescuer
extends an orange slice,
an orange slice, what was he thinking?
while another man holds her, helpless,
in his arms.

Susan Lefler
Brevard, North Carolina

No Woman to Be Rollin

She wasn't there to say goodbye, when last
I was in her house on Lesseps with Sohr

on several walls. It was a baroque room with
a ceiling fan, magazines, books, couches,

a dining room table, chairs, large windows
& a long, long yard on the side. Hot as it

was July, we had comfort, purple chatter
at Lee's "Winter Palace" as Yevtushenko

gawked after the Park, he danced to Louie in
water puddles, snapped his camera, recited

& then to the Lower Ninth Ward. I'll never
we'll never walk that long hallway, a wall of

books, paper, along three large rooms of couches,
beds, lots of odd & mystery cult things in a

New Orleans house you can't find in an
archive, library, or museum. She had family

in Texas, I remind myself, two grown sons
a daughter & a son-in-law, to head start on

misery and loss, awash only in tears, healing
There's no word. The kitchen, it's all gone

No walk out back, that apartment will never
be a theater, again, nor never another poem

will be heard. That is not but charts, digits
for the clean up man, this body has no face

Rudolph Lewis
Jarrett, Virginia

Can You Quilt a Life, Now Dead?

Sharif on the night phone alone, screams
at convention center flood, at superdome
no toilet paper, no diapers, no water, days
cold harsh hearing, "I wish I'd died before . . . ?
wheat, the harvest, the winnowing, are you
greater N'awlins than tribes & families?
Are you 21st c. Israel? Are you wired?
N'awlins, where rise your Little Haiti,
your Vienna, Lower East Side? Forget
Jerusalem, N'awlins more than Louisiana
Let a thousand flowers bloom, N'awlins be
more than a bowl, N'awlins be a spirit quilt

Rudolph Lewis
Jarrett, Virginia

There's No Way Out This Sadness?

Rivers, lakes, and oceans, we've had
aplenty & bayou blues & camelbacks
a Canal Street of tourists & low wages
cultural colonies of Zulus & Mardi Gras
Indians—don't need pen, book, computer
spirit guides, neo-griot, dream masters
There will be no more Treme & Piety
no Desire Street bus & no Gentilly, either
speculators in Benz & Lincoln dealing
cards, situating, photo-oping a life flooded

N'awlins there's no way out this enigma
in a camera, there's no way out this sadness?

Rudolph Lewis
Jarrett, Virginia

Haiku

#1
Love begins slowly
Confusing and abusing
WIND in full motion.

#2
Family, loved sane
Relaxing laughing "oh rain"
Kill steal destroy slain

#3
Soft whistles tips pale
Drip on cement bring rain smell
Smash, crash, everything's Hell.

Shawn Maldon
Washington, District of Columbia

Katrina
In Three Phases
(Gulf Coast Hurricane, August 29, 2005)

I. The Preparation

Provisions gathered
Hibernation formulated
Waiting initiated

Doppler radar screens hold pictures of broken futures
Predictions, instructions, warnings step out
from radio walls

II. The Storm

She screams, battering vacated structures, peopled frames,
and make-shift shelters
She roars, pummeling sea vessels, strong pines, brick
fortresses, surrendered bodies
She quiets, surveying her works through wide-eyed clouds
and left-behind gusts

Observing Nature
Seeing God

III. The Reflection

Gulf Coast sea wind witch
Wind blown power in her arms
Devastating pounding force in her feet
Death blows touching Deep South quadrants

Annihilating human-harnessed powers
Swiping human-inhabited spaces
Contaminating human-consumed necessities
Leaving human-wasted memories

Hours of Fear
Miles of Pieces
Reflections of Lives

Preselfannie Whitfield McDaniels
Jackson, Mississippi

Plane of View

We sent out two plane loads
to San Diego and San Francisco,
twin giant birds jammed with
our dogs and cats. This while
bodies floated like bundles
bounding gently in the toxic gumbo,
and that one in Algiers lay
soaking up sun and fetid air.

I helicoptered over the shifting scene.

These were folk I had seen
sitting on stoops, groups idling at corners, never
amounted to much. Oh, those little ones, childr---

We even got out a parrot.
Ungrateful bird. Here we were
rescuing him, and all he could crack
was "Goddamn your souls to hell!"

Adam David Miller
Berkeley, California

No Occluding the Storm

They walk through rising water,
past floating bodies
and trail ghosts
that elude reporters' cameras
through rites of passage
cannot be swept away
from the city's clutch
as the aftermath drowns
rescue, the rancid decay
rushes into pain-weary eyes.

They did not hear the levees break,
did not hear the watercry
from doors of flooded buildings,
rooftops of broken houses;
still they sift the world
of memory, climb the wavering
limb of hope as another day
cracks the sky, salts open wounds.

Lenard D. Moore
Raleigh, North Carolina

No Relief

We crammed on buses,
jammed into the Superdome
and willed to the mercy
of ourselves, the hot chaos
of the bold Big Easy night
where tension sprouted like lettuce,
swelled like any fertile tomato
and sizzled like cayenne pepper.

We were left like weeds
strewn across the floor,
no water to hydrate, keep us
from wilting in the garden
of ourselves, as imaginary relief
lingered like limitless drought
beneath the busted dome,
no greenhouse to cultivate us.

Lenard D. Moore
Raleigh, North Carolina

Open Note

and we're still finding bodies
shut up in unlivable houses
in the shadow of the Ninth Ward.
we, stricken with sprung roots, face
the salty fact that we're all alone
like desperate kin, weary-eyed.
there were always people perched
on porches because they could;
daylight struck them. even at night,
voices leapt from the porches.
now no words waver on the air,
not the warmth of an adjective,
not the black of a noun,
not the thrust of a verb.
nothing but a band of ghosts
lingering in the breathless place.

Lenard D. Moore
Raleigh, North Carolina

Come Back Ark

We flap like loose shingles
on rooftop after rooftop
listen to ghost helicopters
hover in the thick-black night

We hunker like bullfrogs
We imagine floodwater opening
wide like the wet mouth
of a terror-eyed alligator
tremble to think
of the thunder of its snap
We wonder when the Coast Guard
with boats and life jackets
will plow into the humid throat
of the Gulf Coast night
with rescue-sworn spirits

We want water, purified and cold
and home cooked meals, hot and deep
as the blues we belch
the sweat that drinks us
the way twenty-foot waves swallow

We wait in wartime for National Guard
to search house to house
but the confluence
of fear and grief come first
in the summer of breached laws

We clasp hands as we always have,
though clouds churn and churn.
We cling to communal hope
while all over this place
a foul smell stirs without halt

We avoid wobbling off our haunches;
some of us are vets,
who wait with wounds,
for the Army, Marines, Air Force, Navy
to snatch us before we sink

Lenard D. Moore
Raleigh, North Carolina

A Raging Flood of Tears

they are pulling our dead out of the dead water now
they are pulling our dead out of the dead water now
like they pulled Till out of the Tallahatchie River
and even if we did place the blame where it belongs
would they get off like the men who murdered Emmett?

while reporters blamed us for staying
refusing to see the chains that tied us to the catastrophe
that was to come
like when they tied Malcolm Little's dad
to the tracks
and left him for dead
cause they knew the train was coming

they knew the flood was coming
they knew the levees would break
they were warned
but did nothing
they were warned
but did nothing
they refused to prepare

they are pulling our dead out of the dead water now
counting them as if they were tallying votes
but you cannot measure disgrace with a body-count
and no one wins in death

what have we now but our heartbeats?
and tears
and the whys
of our questions keep coming
even Jesus was said
to have fed the poor
with a few fish and some bread
should we not expect more
from the richest nation
in the history of the world?

scabs are being ripped away
like the homes
revealing old wounds
bleeding sores
infected by the toxic scum
of lies we ingest
as the media contrived words to describe the people
when for five days they were treated like slaves
time warped to the days of whips, chains
and names that were not our own

slave ship screams

ancestors haunt in their hollers for help
in front of cameras that don't care
sending an S.O.S. of sorrow
to a world that looks on in pity and contempt
but hope doesn't stop hunger
and faith can't quench a thirst
mouths parched in the parish
surrounded by water
but can't take a drink

yes, this is hell

the smell of rotting flesh and feces
the stench of death
like Bush's breath hot with deceit
burning under a Louisiana sun
merciless as a slave master
hysterical heat

gnashing teeth, bleeding gums
and the children
the babies delirious with grief

and still they were trapped by the help that would come
abandoned by rescue teams on Highway 10
the help that didn't help
the help that held them hostage
at convention centers that became concentration camps
no refuge
no refuge
no refuge
for the women and their children
and the elders dying in their wheel chairs

smuggled to the super dome that became the prison at
Abu Ghraib
blind-folded by the darkness
and tortured due to the ineptitude of officials
sinking in a cess pool of paranoia
held hostage by helplessness

how long did it take Africans
in texas to learn that they were free?
we know how slow the gov't can be
when it comes to we
who are Black and poor

families again severed
like before
when the auction block was swollen
with our blood and tears
the years are of no consequence
and now we wander the country looking for wives and sons,
daughters and fathers, nanas, poppas,
husbands and cousins and lovers and friends and mothers
and nieces, nephews and ...
tracing the scent of love in hope of embracing them again
on this side
pouring through webpages
hoping to notice a name that sounds like happiness
watching the tv
hoping to recognize a face
that resembles our own
looking for family
longing for home

and I can hear Nina Simone singing
"Mississippi Goddamn Blues"
we who picked cotton there
grew families out of the very ground
we never owned
sucked down gristle just to survive
raised God out the dust bowl
and blew life into our bodies
with nothing
nothing
nothing
but the defiant desire to live
and once more nothing is all we have
but the defiant desire to live again
resurrected like the Jeez that is us
who will march a jazz dirge
on down Bourbon Street
to honor those whose bodies still float in the 9th Ward?

who will rebuild the city
that city of saints and haints?
bring the reconstruction that never came
after Lee surrendered the war

jim crow knows
let trent lott rot in the rubble of his plantation mansion
for all those that perished unnecessarily

yes there is anger
a raging flood of tears

Bush looted our taxes
sent them overseas
robbed our rights
cracked presidential jokes as the smoke still rose
"the soft bigotry of low expectations" is Bush's to claim
a smug racism he learned on his mother's knee

yes the U.S. is a Third World nation
no corporate press can cover the truth now
where dictators lie, cheat and steal
then kill the poor that would defy them
the emperor has no clothes
his ass is exposed
been stripped naked by his own shame
time to name names

there is a raging flood headed right to the White House
and FEMA can't rescue you now

what has happened here is a crime
the homicide of an entire city

hear the prophecy my ancestors sung
God showed Noah
by the rainbow sign
said it wont be water but fire next time

the flames are burning!

Ewuare Osayande
Philadelphia, Pennsylvania

Katrina

Babies in the river
who leapt from Mother's arms
Swim down Bourbon Street
twenty years early.
Above the banks
survivors scan rooftops
for displaced diamonds,
pan gutters for trinkets
to store in soggy pockets.
While in their bellies
Ecoli swim to a new surface
to divide and redivide
reincarnate and reinhabit
beneath the skin of the
desperately thirsty.
And tonight the pine caskets
will rise and burst forth
bleached bones—
reclaim the streets
that were once theirs
and welcome the dead
to submerge this fetid land.

Laurel Peterson
Carlisle, Pennsylvania

Take me away

Take me away from this stench where
I was born
Where the walls have swollen and mold
has grown
Take me away from my cats in their
corner.
Their eyes are filled with fear and the
darkness of the water.
Take me away from spray painted X's
that mark the doors.
They whisper "life here will be forgotten
and left in ruins to this war."

Stephen Rooney
Baltimore, Maryland

Drowning

Our wings are clipped
We cannot fly north
Home is a ruin
Sucked dry by a dark pool
That has left nothing but crumbs
Crumbs to bring to my nest
Crumbs that are guarded by crows
Hunters darker than water
who used these crumbs as bait
They hook us in from their towers
Day after day, I risk my life
In search for these crumbs so my
family can survive
I was able to hide from them again today
but I know they will soon find me
They will raid my nest,
        take my children away

Nights are restless here
In this pit I once called home
The crows are killing each other
again
And their fires continue to grow
They have found us
Their heads are being forced through
my door.
Sharp beaks fly by me and drill into
my wall
My family is part of this decay.
The darkness will consume us.
There is no Escape.

Stephen Rooney
Baltimore, Maryland

Katrina

Forecasts.
Sirens.
Cries.
Winds rushed to New Orleans,
Splashing water did not discriminate,
Black and white bodies floated,
Yellow busses rested miles away
Until Katrina left town.
The Mayor spoke
The Governor spoke
The President spoke
Too late.

Leonard A. Slade, Jr.
Albany, New York

Survived

Chaos surrounds me, Fear enters my soul
Darkness swallows every inch of light across the horizon
The earth's deep-rooted limbs sway and crack in the path
of harsh whispers
I see no one, I hear no one
No one sees me, No one hears me . . . she's coming

The powerful beat of the slave drums echo in the air
A powerful spirit of a black woman is approaching
She journeys from the world of old—of past
Hungry for punishment, Thirsty for revenge
She satisfies her appetite as she steps from the water onto
the land
With her arms, she brings the liquids of the earth
All connected from its four sources...she stands

As her mouth opens, hatred pours like a waterfall
So much, so deep, so harsh, so powerful
Her targets are the states where her ancestors died
The states that presented their slaves
with the ultimate gift
She fires
Every emotion liquid death
Unseen...She fights

I see death in the mist of waters
I feel tears in the presence of adversity
I hear the pains of the people
I taste the bitterness and sourness of her mind
I smell the odor of a now damaged nation...she smiles

So much destruction exists
Liquid life now owns a blended culture
Dark is a region so friendly
What once was bright and colorful is now dark and grim
Life no longer exists
I cry, she cries, the world cries
She smiles, she frowns—mixed emotions
She comes, she stands, she fights, she smiles
She leaves...Another new day!

Samanthia Nicole Thompson
Vicksburg, Mississippi

History in the water

The policeman takes dog
from young boy's hands
Snowball he cries
eyelashes rain

> a man holds his wife and son
> son and wife
> water storms the steeples
> she says: *let me go*
> he does: grief streaming

woman with skin dressed in wrinkles
rocks on a superdome cot
people flood the stadium
three now beside her waiting
no blood between them

soldier calls home to Biloxi
CNN his only connection
water drowns phone lines
dust hijacks his memories of safety
he grounds the butt of his gun in the sand

Bush views bottom of a slave ship
from his bubble in the sky
terrorists take notes
Black people still traveling
middle passage on buses

Rosa Parks stands up
her spoken word to the wind
blow to the middle of the sea
save these brave people from your hot moods

The next world war will be about water.

Becky Thompson
Jamaica Plain, Massachusetts

Tell me this is not my america

Tell me this is not my america
     where the trees snapped
     and the walls caved in;
               rain water
swirled and all the colors bled into one
     stains of yellow honey—
     burnt dark orange whiskey—
     bright green
         tight
         algae—
     draining down
coupling with the mud of the mississip
filling up the sewers so fast
the pumps just had to break;
               the sound
of mad belching machines; the sound
of sizzling and frying; the sound of a high
crying whine fit for a graveyard was the
sound of all jazz bands
in the world
crying. The city of music was drowned:
black water curled around toes,
black water poured in the windows.
black water crept up the slippery steps.
black water licked the beams, and yet,
the first thing I hear is well, why in the
hell didn't they just leave?

Tell me this is not my america.
slogging knee deep
again
in a morass of skin that is deeper
than skin because it permeates
down to the bones, it
seeps into our sweet red marrow

Tell me this is not my america,
a howling rage of a blackened voice
that is too poor to be heard,
while the haves and the rich
and the whites with the prime land
on the crescent slices of the moon
              cocoon themselves in
and count only the primes of their bank
accounts full of prime numbers burning
sublime
with cars as big as boats
            and yachts and planes

Tell me this is not my america where they
            simply drove away
and who cared for what was left
because Barbara B said it's ok
you must know the only ones left
are the darkest dregs.

Tell me this is not my america
where houses poked through
the sea of stinking water
like rafts
and people chewed holes
through their ceilings, their
rafters, their shingles, to stand
alone, in pairs, under the brooding sky
scattering bits of kibble for the cats
and the dogs like little drops of hope
for a family member almost sure
to die alone, in the water, or starve,
a thin skeleton, another skin of crying
            children saying goodbye

Tell me this is not my america
where the rain doesn't pour down
for forty days or nights
but there's a flood just the same
and then the sky goes silent
           still
                not a drop of rain
not even so much as a rainbow
and certainly no sounds of
any planes... Tell me, tell me,

Tell me please, this is not my america,
where coffins pop up and drift down
the river again
strange boats indeed.

Chris Vierck
Lenoir, North Carolina

The Day When They Stopped the Music

White picket fences
transposed into wrought iron gates
neither can hold back
the sky
if it decides to
sneeze & cough
on the carbon freely
released by the spincters
of a million metal roaches
with no fear of the light
or any GOD
while we smoke the rainforest
& greedily drink the polar ice cap
survival of the highest & driest
federalized private armies
guard oil fields & bank vaults
with our teapot dome being supersized
a huge mass enmassed
with similar hues
why are so many blotted bodies
old & poor & decolored
don't even let them eat cake
what was saved
for this rainy day
damn the dams &
level the levees
as they level play grounds
for so many of the dammed
eroded big easy, so easily
as the 9th ward was
underwater in the side pocket

brownie's fema fear was fatal
cronies to the bone
awashed in bad blood to the bone
as no one could cell phone home
halos in the shape of helios
beating blades
lower floors rinsed
of memories
historic artifacts
are on 2 wet legs now
headlines devalued nature &
upped the ante

for those still in attics
waiting.

Willie Williams
Detroit, Michigan

My Soul is Anchored

NEW ORLEANS STREET MEMORIES–

I REMEMBER THE STREETS OF NEW ORLEANS —
MARDI GRAS DAY
STREET PARADES WINDING THEIR WAY-- THROUGH
THE BROAD BOULEVARDS BRIMMING WITH THE BOLD
COLORS OF PASSING FLOATS
STREET PERFORMERS IN BRIGHT PURPLES AND RED
PANTOMIMING-- JUGGLING
BRASS BANDS STRUTTING WITH CROWDS
SECONDLINING
STREET PEDDLERS HAWKING SHINY METALLIC
JEWELS — LUSCIOUS LUCKY DOGS
BOYS BOJANGLING ON BOURBON STREET SIDEWALKS
FOR A FEW TOSSED COINS
ARTISTS PAINTING PICTURESQUE STREET SCENES IN
JACKSON SQUARE FROM DAWN TO DUSK.

RIDING THE OLD STREETCARS, YOU CAN HEAR
THE CONDUCTOR'S CRY AS IF JOINED WITH THE
CLANGING OF THE TROLLEY:
CANAL STREET! RAMPART ST!
BASIN ST! BOURBON ST!
DESIRE ST!—A STREETCAR NAMED DESIRE--
DESIRE STREET!
SOMEWHERE ON THESE STREETS YOU CAN HEAR
BLANCHE DUBOIS RECITING:

"They told me to take a street-car named Desire, and
transfer to one called Cemeteries, and ride six blocks and
get off at—Elysian Fields!"—Elysian Fields or The Champs
Elysees? No –Elysian Fields...
A bus has replaced the Streetcar named Desire
 It runs straight through the quarter, past the old market
places , over city bridges, traversing miles across town until
it reaches the end of its run in the Ninth Ward, lined with
shotgun palaces
The soon-to-be -gentrified nine— home to a neighborhood
named Desire—now little more than a town of ghosts.

Caffin Ave! Charbonnet St! Lamanche St! Lizardi St! Flood
St! What will become of this street and all of those houses
where the waters rose to the rafters?
Flood St. a Lower 9 landmark of sorts —ravaged and ripped
apart by Katrina
Did you know that Sister Zora spent time in the Lower 9
studying spiritualist traditions under Mother Catherine?
Streets that mark boundaries of this now-completely
devastated area dominate Zora's folksy declaration of how to
get to Mother Catherine's church:

   "One must go straight out St. Claude St below the
Industrial Canal and turn south on Flood St. and go almost
to the Florida Walk. A marsh lies between Flood St. and that
flag-flying enclosure and one must walk. As one approaches,
the personality of the place comes out to meet one. No
ordinary person created this thing."

Claiborne Avenue! Touro St ! Pauger St !Marigny St! Marais
St! ---I imagine hearing Sister Zora ask
"Which way to Marais St?"
And as she anticipates finding her way, she hears singing-
"Hey pocky -way—Tu way pocky- way"
Got to find a way to Marais—Got to see the Indians come
out
dancing and singing their street ditties
cuz "It's Carnival Time and Everybody's Drinking Wine."

Lena Marie Ampadu
Towson, Maryland

Voodoo Goeth

A city once carrying a
Spell at the hands of Laveau,
Now departed, having fled
Ahead of the whir of
Trampling feet.
What a pity...pity...pity.

Bruce Baker
Henderson, Nevada

Attic

Dear Lawd, Dear Lawd
De water's comin
In dis bowl we sit
Too late for runnin

I planted fields
I plowed de lan
I'll drop right hea
Right where I stan

From de Lower Nine
To Rampart Street
Water creeps up my window
Past my tired feet

Tried cookin and playin
In a Marching band
Sung songs of plenty
About this Carnival lan

My soul is tired
Just like befo
Grown sick and tired
Can't cry no mo

When the water's gone
And up come de tree
Up in dis attic
Is where I'll be.

Bruce Baker
Henderson, Nevada

Lost and Found

My home lost as the water rose to the roof
and I waited for my rescue then
long days and nights at the superdome
with no food or water
Help comes
O Thank you, Lord
as I found my spirit to go on
to find a new home, new friends
and a cozy bed

Emily Cadden
Roanoke, Virginia

this just in

the lowest hell hymns a third
world war   one million people
packed in tempers
burrowed beneath homes since 1974

before the gulf migrates to men

dissie for miles
celebrating teeth on brass

beignets uptown
best with beverage

> manufactured mystery
> to a twelve year old's *why?*

>> *a little lagniappe, hear*
>> *a little lagniappe, hear*

hurried its *pissed* performance

severed scenes

> delivering youth

> kneeling soul
> sipping sin

> igniting self
> slapping laughter

a little lagniappe, hear
a little lagniappe, hear

Delicia Daniels
Marshall, Texas

Dear New Orleans:
~ for the poets who write the city

wonder where the poets are
who used to poet here
made love to the Gulf that swallowed
every syllable whole

mass deconstruction of sentence
structures built
now buried in the belly of a strange
woman who made no introduction
Katrina

jazz city, creole nation, griot gumbo
no bread crumbs to lead you back home
you—did not get lost
somebody let your writing hand go
slipped then adrift

de-settled like
dust tracks on a road
where have your words gone
maybe dropped in the Industrial Canal
with the weight of the world tied to each letter

tried to drown your sound like
Emmett Till in the bottom of the Mississippi
to surface at the deep end
doing the back stroke
the butterfly the
breast stroke

because of your words
the Crescent City lives
it beats it keeps

Deborah D. Grison
Union City, New Jersey

Lullaby

when the gulf of Mexico stretches his arms
lays his head on Easy levees
bodies rest under blankets of water
as Louis sings a lullaby
that fills their ears like wrinkled water

Melanie Henderson
Washington, District of Columbia

God's Little Reality Check

The beginning of the end, all in one.
The short-lived beginning of the experience
that left an everlasting ending.

All the material possessions that once meant so much,
Now taken, out of reach, out of touch.
The lives of so many, removed from this earth
Released to a place of constant rebirth.

The hurt, the tear, and devastation of having
to start a new life.
Who knows, maybe everything will be okay, maybe
a second chance would be nice.

Now here we are in a state of shock, marked
by a reality that I just can't mentally block.
Forced to take a step towards a place that's
completely not me, and constantly told to just "let it be."

An immediate rush of uncertainty fills my mind.
Who to turn to? Who will listen?
Who will simply take the time
news flash, after news flash, echoing in my head.
A constant reminder of the day
that ripped our lives to shreds.

Gabrielle High
Vicksburg, Mississippi

Little Black Ballerina in Mississippi Clay

Before Katrina's Kiss

she pushes her doubts
with flat palms
on tipped toes
she is always dancing
walking on sunshine
running from clouds

heaven is a dark today
god must be grey
she focuses on her steps
blinded by the rays of Dawn
between her black toes
her feet blistered by the brilliance
of her buried ancestors

she dances on their graves
and gardens, overgrown,
using a heel toe method
planting her fate
in sacred soil
it blooms like wild flowers
bright red blotchy promises
of beauty

she twirls and whistles
the melody of her name
in the wind
to accompany
the wings of her soul

Damaris Beecher Hill
Towson, Maryland

Saving Ourselves

She started as rain, picked up her speed,
and turned into a deadly hurricane.

When she hit, some peoples' lives were
affected, but many lives were forever
changed.

She entered their town, knocked their
houses, cars, and other things around,
Now it seems as if their world is
upside down.

They called her Katrina, a hurricane
that had many people chasing
FEMA.

For some she took everything,
for many she took few.
However, our main concern was
how long it took to rescue.

We moved to other areas and
states, and became evacuees.
How could television label us
as the term "refugees?"

It took a week to get there,
and many people died. BET had
a marathon titled "Saving Ourselves",
because George Bush doesn't care
if we are alive!

Doretha S. Jackson
Pearl, Mississippi

The Test

She came with little warning,
like a thief in the night.
But who are we to say
that the timing wasn't right.
She destroyed homes and took lives
but she never harmed our will to survive.
Was she a curse or a blessing in disguise?
Was this a test to see if the Nation would rise?
Was Katrina the worst or was it her aftermath?
Was it Louisiana and Mississippi's destiny to be in her path?
Given the circumstance it's hard to tell.
But if it was a test did we pass or fail?

Katina Johnson
Vicksburg, Mississippi

from a hill far away

they thought they
heard a
thimble of spit
whisper: (pling)
upon hitting—

but from where they
were sitting
the thrash of
hammering drink
had no sting,
no fury

and so,
not to worry,
they thought

(until some of them were called to pray and stand
where their own were fed to earth)

Ladianne Henderson Mandel
Charlotte, North Carolina

I Remember You, Biloxi

Before the crashing of Camille
I remember you, Biloxi.
You seventeenth century jewel
Of live oak cathedrals
Dripping Spanish moss
Of churches and garden paths
Smelling musty with age
Of azaleas and camellias
Blooming in winter.

Before the cacophony of casinos
I remember you, Biloxi,
When long vistas were unobstructed
By gaming barges
When my serene gaze
Drifted seamlessly
From stately homes
To white sand stretches
And finally to the sea.

Before the coup de grace of Katrina
I remember you, Biloxi,
For June's blessing of the fleet
Whose boats chugged out at dawn
And returned in red sunset.
Only the lighthouse remains
Making me believe
In resurrection.

Jan McGregor
Booneville, Mississippi

A Song for N'Awlins

I want to sing a song for New Orleans...
Of the neutral zones of Tremé and Gert Town...
Sing a song for Rampart Street and Congo Square
where everyday is a history lesson.
Sing a song for my ancestors Alexander, Sarah, Ellis Hughes.

I wished I had told her that she was the only one...
That filled my heart with its lassiere faire
and living in extremes ...
That sometimes is too hard to bear, the in your face,
with so much life and verve and noise.
And the music, the music, that bubbled up
in the cracks of the promenade
Where the cadence in bottle caps
on sneakers of youn'uns crying
"Throw me a coin, mister"

And the "Don't worry bebe"
And having champagne and grits at midnight.
Sing a song for Dunbar's and Dooky Chase,
Hubig pies and Blue Bonnet Ice Cream...
On those hot humid days that make you scream...
Me scream...
We all scream for ice cream.
"Where love is like a card game,
you only have to deal it once"

There were no refugees here, only hardworking,
tax paying citizens who held up
A redolent city sometimes with sheer grit
and determination
Sing a song also for St Bernard and Jefferson Parish
in water flowing deep
In the eyes of a man who could only weep
at the death of a mother
Who waited for her son to come and get her?
Give a field holler for Port Gibson, Biloxi,
Gulfport, Oxford, Jackson
And the Mississippi Delta
for the blues that came up out of the fields.
For all the ones that say...
"Where yer at? And " for true?"

Shout out for the Panorama Jazz Band and Hector...
For Mrs. Baptist and Mrs. Sanders spending
a quiet afternoon catching up on the latest local yore
And Tony's to die for barbecue and his
"Fo' sho! Greeting you.
And my dear hearts Ed and Tony whose hearts and souls are
incomparable who was there always there.
And Snug Harbor (one and two).
And C. Ray Nagin, Eddie Compass
and all the rest you are the best.

Sing a song for the ones who were treated like gum
stuck on the bottom of a dog's paw ...
When the chips were down
For people who wanted to know who your mama was rather
then asked you how much you made.
Sing a song for Roysalis, Sammy Lee, Aunty Ruth
and Donovan, Chief Tootie, CAC and NOCCA.
And all the "Yeah you right"
that have not yet been declared.
The White Linen Nights...
The zydeco...

Second Lines not yet boogie woogie to.
For boudin ...
And po'boys
And poor people who could not afford anything else
And could not flee because they had no place to go.

Tell the story of Novelle d'Orleans
where for an evening it was a place where care forgot...
And for Xavier, Suno, Dillard and the Amistad...
For praline pies and real crab cakes, crawfish ...
And African people who knew the difference
between Creole and Cajun...
And whose souls intertwined in the soils...
The Ashanti, the Gambian, the Senegalese
and the Wolof who knew dafuskie...

For the 1.5 million who are standing on the shores...
(Even here in Greensboro)
Watching their homes and their lives...
And their history swallowed up by the lies of thugs...
Rampant shootings...
And "lawless New Orleans"

Sing the songs of Jelly Roll, Louis Armstrong,
Gate Mouth, the Nevelle Brothers, Buddy Bolden, Wynton
Marsalis, Harold Baptist, Marva Wright,
Danny Barker, Kid Creole, Mardi Gras Indians
Andrew Young, and Marc Morial ...
And Fats Domino *who found his thrill in New Orleans*
Where jazz is the democracy wrapped up in music.

Sing a song for New Orleans
making her dramatic exit as we once knew her...
Stage left embraced for a moment in the watery arms of the
mighty, mighty Mississippi.
As the Ponchatrain claims its own.
A second line for the beignets, pralines...
3rd Ward, 13th Ward, 7th Ward and the Lower Nines.

For the ones who were reunited today
and the ones still missing.
Herald a joyful noise full with beignets, café au lait,
Jazzfest and Bayou Classic
And Essence Music Festival
Aie!
Le Bon Temps Rouler!
(Let the good times roll)

Jacquelyn Hughes Mooney
Greensboro, North Carolina

Caveat Emptor

We have danced, we have loved
we have built our coffins
in the eyes of storms.
These winds and waters rise and wane.
Our truths are simple ones:
We wait on a god
Who holds in his left fist Pain
In his right palm, Goodness.

We batten our eyes and hum
the below- sea- level-blues.
This land is ours bought and paid
In our flesh and loves rended,
In our rents, paid cash—
We hold these beauties to be self evident
As red beans and rice and lottery dreams,
As beaded memories.

Settle down now, and wait on The Lord!
Scheduled to arrive in four more days
by helicopter, those chopping blades
Troubling troubling the waters below
Coming, just as soooon, soon as He sniffs
The smoke signals
From NPR, CBS, NBC, ABC, FOX and
The nattering blogosphere nabobs.

But that 2nd coming will be too late
The bell's already been rung
And Richard Baker says
the jig is up. Yep, say the *corpse
of engineers,* the party's over. Their levee broke a tooth
and through the gap spat everything we bought
With our blood, with our Blues, with our
Satchelmouth laughter, with our black
face shrugs and softshoe,
with our Buffalo Soldiers and salty tears
for Negro Heroes, for our back
of the bus, our sitting downs,
our snacks at the Woolworth's,
our Martins, Tuskegees and lynchability.

Once more we march
leave home and hearth.
There's some deep memory here—
Once more our shores shrink
from hungry view,
our dead swallowed up
by the waters.

But just you wait
wait wait on the Lord!
He is a revelation
in the receding flood waters—
FEMA water bottles, photo albums,
bald tires, blasted bibles and floating fecal treasures,
in refrigerators
curb leaning like the broken teeth
of a battered goddess
their mouths full of dirty secrets,
taped shut.

But every violence speaks its own language.
Listen to the ice box, leaning
at the corner of Desire and Abundance
talking back like the stone tablets of Moses
or a Rosetta rock, its graffiti message
gives a single commandment
from the Creator of All New Disasters:
"Caveat, Do Not enter."

Oh, Listen! the King of the Zulus is
Not dead. He is trumpeting a line
To Congo Square from the lower 9.
This time we know the names of the lost.
We know the land of our mothers.
We enter. Against all warning.
We remain. Inconstant as memory. Powerful
As a storm.

Opal Moore
Atlanta, Georgia

Dear God

It used to be
I would fall to the floor and press my forehead to it
in moments of despair

I would say help me
help me

but listen
I am ok
but I just now found myself pressing my forehead
to the carpet of my stairs

about the waters in the flooded cities
poisoned by oilspill, chemicals, the dead
about the survivors forever traumatized
dear god
I am alive I am alive
help them

Alicia Ostriker
Princeton, New Jersey

I wanna be an evacuee: the Barbara Bush blues

The ditty about the Crescent City
for you to read in a little hush
it came alive after some jive
from the mouth of Barbara Bush...

"So many of the [displaced] people in the arena here, you know, were
underprivileged anyway, so this – this is working very well for them."

– Barbara Bush, former first lady and mother of a president,
September 2005

Poor people everywhere:
hope for disaster, pestilence, flood,
pray for mudslides, earthquakes, wildfires –
that's when the going really gets good!

Pray to be flushed out of your home –
watch it float away to rot;
pray to end up in the Astrodome
on a blue Red Cross cot.

Away from the hood, you get nutritious food
and free dental care;
you get coupons to hoity-toity salons
that can comb the goop from your hair.

You get clean clothes, deodorant soap
and warm water to wash;
you get all this and every little wish –
plus a tidy bit of cash.

True, you may lose some of your little bums
or your minimum-wage job,
but these are just blips: after the apocalypse
you live high on the hog.

So, clasp your hands now and pray to join the thousands
living large and scot-free!
They've got it so swell I think that, well,
I might just become an evacuee.

Rohan Preston
Golden Valley, Minnesota

Ms. Diane

I would often drift into your garden
Now and then to hear your wind chimes
Every lost loved one had their chime
Each sang a different song
The wind would lead them in a dance
The breeze would guide as they would follow
But then one day the wind turned
violent and chimes were left torn
and tangled.
The trees lay to rest with your loved ones.
Your garden cannot hold the victims
of this tragedy.
Now we must find the branches
to take in a thousand more.

Stephen Rooney
Baltimore, Maryland

The Big Easy Blues

This wonderful thing called life, just ain't fair,
This wonderful thing called life, just ain't fair.
You see, people lie and they cheat, and when ends don't meet,
no one is around to care.

Innocent people have too much to bear,
Innocent people have too much to bear.
The thing is, these people don't lie, and they don't cheat,
and still, no one is around to care.

Not just houses, but homes were torn apart,
Not just houses, but homes were torn apart,
The buildings that held laughter and tears lost their hearts.

They say down south, the wind is sweeter,
They say down south, the wind is sweeter.
Why, oh why, then...did Katrina beat her?

Some saw it comin', and had no place to go
Some saw it comin', and had no place to go.
Now they're left sayin':
life just ain't easy in the Big Easy no mo'.

Emily Schrecker
Herndon, Virginia

Untitled

Still, quiet, was the calm
Before the storm approached
To pierce our souls, grab our hearts
And upon our lives encroach.
Flooded streets, razed homes,
Innumberable children left alone,
Wailing winds in choral fashion,
Drenching rains and lightning flashing.
Few are those without a story
Of Katrina and her glory.

Dark, dismal, was the day
when she arrived in all her splendor
Bending trees, flying debris
Twirled 'round as in a blender.
Nervous stomachs and frightened eyes
Beheld the turmoil of the skies
No field, no stadium or arena
Could contain our mourning of Katrina.

Steven Shadwick
Vicksburg, Mississippi

To Whom It May Concern

Dear F.E.M.A.:

This is Brotha Hustle applying for a job with your organization. I figure if Mr. Brown can get a job with ya, so can I. Please check out my resume!

Brotha Hustle
Aunt Tee-Tees Place
1717 Around-the-Corner St.
Way-'Cross, Ga., 34777
707-777-9311.

Objective: To obtain gainful employment in the field of emergency management with the possibility of earning extra money by providing food, water, shoes, clothes, Juicy Juice on ice (for the kids) and other necessities to flood and hurricane victims.

Work Experience/Qualifications: 2000 to present: Self-employed (Hustler). Vendor on various street corners.

2004 to present: Clubb Chicken Wing Security. Temporary/part-time security guard during Sunday Nite Bingo.

2003 to 2004: Cootie Creek County Sanitation Department. Refurbished, recycled and re-sold hundreds of unneeded items, such as discarded clock radios, busted video cassette players, used phone cards and old perfume, ties, hats, shirts, etc.

2002 to 2003: Cootie Creek County Middle School Night Custodian. Cleaned toilet stalls, mopped floors, wiped windows, picked up trash.

2001 to 2002: After I lost my good factory job with benefits, I sold government cheese, butter and powdered milk—at reasonable prices—to people who really needed these food items.

Education: Cootie Creek County Community College's GED Program. Certificate of Ghetto Science Vocational Education and Critical Thinking and S.O.H.K. (School of Hard Knocks).

References Available Upon Request.

By: Freelance on Sept 21, 05

Ken Stiggers
Jackson, Mississippi

Help Is On The Way!
September 28, 2005

It's time for "Rescue 911 is a Joke" with Flava-Flav: "Yeah boyeeeee! Check out this phone call between Mayor Ray Nagin of New Orleans and Sis Ernestine, the Emergency Operator."
Ernestine answers phone after 10 ringy dingies: "Snort ... This is Ernestine. How may I help you?"

Ray Nagin: "This is the mayor of New Orleans with an urgent request for help. While these floodwaters rise, crackheads need a fix, sick folk are dying, and people need food and water. It's awful down here. I need reinforcements, troops, buses, everything!

Ernestine: "Mr. Naggin, sir ..."

Ray Nagin: "That's Nagin, not Naggin!"

Ernestine: "I'm sorry, Mr. Naggin. The president, vice president and secretary of state are vacationing, and FEMA is BRAINSTORMING—excuse my pun—with the National Guard. ... Snort!"

Ray Nagin: "Miss Ernestine, your jokes are tired. If something doesn't happen now, I'm gonna get rowdy, loud and BLACK! You feel me?"

Ernestine: "Hold your horsies, Mr. Naggin! Help is on the way! And remember: Long distance is the next best thing to being there. ... Snort! Snort!"

Frustrated Ray Nagin: "Aw crap! Don't tell me people are coming here! They're not here! It's too doggone late. Now get off you're @SS and do something, and let's fix the biggest GODD@MN crisis in the history of this country!!!" (Nagin hangs up the phone.)

Ernestine watches Wolf Blitzer of CNN News report on Hurricane Katrina victims.

Ernestine: "My, those poor people are sooo black."

By: Freelance on Sept 28, 05

Ken Stiggers
Jackson, Mississippi

Another Phoenix

Looking up from television
four years later,
still envisioning those tall towers
on fire/burning
crumbling under the weight of terrorism
engulfing so many lives
for some a turning point occurred
in time beyond the pain/tears
stubbornly stopping years later
still hoping there was no one personally known
who saw the planes
felt the crash
said good-bye
died that day
Once again
the events we are compelled to recall
Where were you...? becomes a mutual greeting
Now,
Katrina forces us again
to trust God more/seek inner peace
while a city lays victim to nature
politics shows its aversion to poverty
Babylon distortions are recited
New Orleans will rise again
above the countless tragedies
beyond the horrors nature created
sympathy prevails
"by the grace..."
So we give till our own rent is due
gas prices force us to stay home captivated
watching numbness become the new pastime
with each newscast/telethon
a FEMA Director learns the perils of padding a
resume
when destruction becomes verification

On this day two tragedies collide
Some take a deep breath
while others continue healing somewhere devils don't
value a poet's verbs
stopping long enough to sense a cool breeze at
Summer's end
Fall awaits its turn
seasons are cyclical under a perfect sky
silently a chant is born/becoming a remedy...
those colorful Mardi Gras beads she used to wear
Someday the lady will greet a spirited visitor again
on some Fat Tuesday
laissez les bon temps rouler
("Let the good times roll")

Laissez les Bon Temps Rouler,
Again!

Aissatou Sunjata
Fayetteville, North Carolina

Katrina

A poem about the impact of this hurricane on the disadvantaged...

Katrina
eased up in the gulf
the gulf of Mexico
warm waters of that tropic sea
built dat bitch strong for show

Katrina
set her sights upon
them bayou delta towns
mud puppy eatin cajun folk
their smiles now are frowns

Katrina
grew to level five
slowed down to level foe
she hit them delta towns so hard....
them towns ain't there no moe

Katrina...
busted levees, blew down trees,..
had delta folk down on they knees!
cryin jesus, god, somebody please!
deliver us from this disease!
don't leave us in the mud!
but...

Katrina....
plague like did descend
with driving rain and torrential wind...
and in her wake, a flood
rich folks fled to higher ground
poor folks climbed up on they roof ...
with the pudding comes the proof

Katrina...
came for blood

Katrina
left the delta poor
all stranded in the dark
homeless, helpless, wet and scared
four days without the least bit shared
feelin like nobody cared
George Bush flew by and stared

Katrina
is a testament of poverty and greed
it personifies the vast divide
between those that have
and those that need

so how shall we proceed?

Steven G. Taylor
St. Petersburg, Florida

After the Hurricanes
(for the radical writers in New Orleans)

Poverty is not devoid of its dignity,
Nor is the Ninth Ward a fractured mirror
For minor gods to behold factitious laughter.
Beware of aliens, of inside agitators, of vultures
Who would batten on grief and broken hearts,
Kidnap our cultures and dreams, wondrously aged,
Transport and auction them for abuse.
Against such tragedy within tragedy we stand
In solidarity for life, for liberty, for return to happiness.

Saints and soldiers creative
Be not blindly meditative,
Seeking at noon
An impossible drinking gourd.

Hope is not devoid of its deceit,
Nor immune to misleading into swamps.
Careful. Don't move left. Quicksand be there.
Don't move right. Gators will kiss you.
Learn from the fugitive enslaved.
Befriend moccasins.
Capture and coffle the cruel,
The arrogant, the mammon cold.
Send them on middle passages into the blues.

Jerry W. Ward, Jr.
New Orleans, Louisiana

Rage

Rage against the night and darkness
     Is needful . . .
     To shine light on our own path—
     Once it is gone
     We begin to see in the dark and
          can help others find their way in
          dark places as well.

Jane Watts
Madison, Mississippi

Katrina: Ancestral Call

Louie Armstrong, your trumpet must be blowing
for the anguish of your people
Sarah Vaughn, please moan for those
who can't seem to utter a sound
Duke Ellington, let your hands run across the keys
To tinkle the sound of tears from those lost in starvation
Lady Day, cry out in soft tones
As you did when you sang Strange Fruit
There was bitter fruit in New Orleans
As folks begged for food and hung in lines for hours
Count Basie, play those chords and hum along
To soothe the anguish of Motherless children

Saints of New Orleans, march down those muddy streets
Playing your instruments to cleanse the toxicity
of racism and neglect
Play hard and loud in your funeral march
To comfort those bodies who lay on the streets for days
All musicians who have gone from the French Quarters
To a better place Beyond
Spread a blanket of comfort for those who still remain
Like Fats Domino who had to be carried out to safety

Martin and Malcolm, lead us out to find a better place
And remind us when we become complacent
Medgar Evers and Fannie Lou Hamer, give us the Word
To stand before the delegates and say, "We must be heard!"
W.E.B. DuBois and Frederick Douglass, remind us to stand up
and orate and record our history
So this will not be forgotten!
Sojourner and Phillis Wheatley, lead us to freedom
And help us to create the poems that say,
"We can't be turned around!"
Help us to bring forth those who will stand tall!

We need warriors to come forth and say,
    "We will not allow our bodies to be stacked up again
    like our ancestors were in ships."
We need children and young people to walk forward and say,
    "We want the best education and we need nurturing so
    we can grow to be strong adults
    to fight the system bravely!"
We need all allies: Black and White, Native and Latino,
Asian and East Indians, Gay and Straight, Rich and Poor to
stand together and say,

    "We see the Racism and we will not allow it
    to happen anymore."
    "We see it and our eyes can't be closed any longer!"
    "We see the poor and disenfranchised and
    will not allow that anymore!"
    "We will pull together so that All people will be free!"
    "All men and women will have quality of life and
    will not be ignored and treated with disrespect!"

We need to stand together and march forth
To show the strength of our convictions and shout,
No more! No more! You will not do this to us anymore!
This time it's out there and you can't sweep it
under the rug of power and greed
It won't stay under there anymore!
This must NEVER happen again!
No more! No more!

H.E.R. Ward
Charlottesville, Virginia

Acknowledgments

This collection, *Mourning Katrina: A Poetic Response to Tragedy* is on one level the result of a very personal response to a public tragedy. I, like so many other Americans, desperately wanted to do something to help in the wake of Hurricane Katrina, a storm that affected the lives of millions of people on the Gulf Coast. However, the book really owes its existence to the cooperation and generosity of spirit of more than three hundred people who participated in the Mourning Katrina National Poetry Writing Project.

For me the tragedy had a very familiar face. Many of the friends of Furious Flower were caught up in the disaster: former Louisiana Poet Laureate Brenda Marie Osbey, Kalamu ya Salaam and his wife Nia, Jerry Ward, Jr., Quo Vadis Gex-Breaux, Sybil Kein, and Mona Lisa Saloy, among others. Kalamu was among the first to appeal to the writers' community to help in any way it could. Jerry Ward, who evacuated to Vicksburg, Mississippi, made a major contribution by submitting the poems of more than 20 students to this project. Brenda Marie Osbey lifted our spirits with her determination that New Orleans would live again.

The initial aim of the Mourning Katrina National Writing Project was to help survivors deal with the emotional trauma of their experience through writing poetry. The first positive outcome was that those who submitted their poems had their work read by noted poets and teachers. Among those who volunteered to respond to these writers were: Elizabeth Alexander, Marvin Broome, Daryl Dance, Miriam De Costa Willis, Toi Derricotte, Nikki Giovanni, Sandra Govan, Maryemma Graham, Trudier Harris, Everett Hoagland, Hilary Holladay, Malaika Albrecht King, Tony Medina, Adam David Miller, Opal Moore, jessica care moore, Eugene Redmond, Sonia Sanchez, Tiwanna Simpson, Chezia

Thompson Strand, Judith Thomas, and Jerry Ward, Jr. I am indebted to them for their kindness.

We, at the Furious Flower Poetry Center, gratefully acknowledge all those who contributed poems to the Mourning Katrina project. Approximately 200 children and adults submitted poems and narratives to the project. We are grateful for their written permission to use the poems in this volume. Several people assisted us in getting these submissions. We wish to thank the teachers and administrators at Lee High in Baton Rouge, Louisiana; Jacquelyn Cummings, Guidance Counselor, at West Baltimore Middle School #80 in Baltimore, Maryland; Chezia Thompson Cager Strand at the Maryland Institute College of Art; and William Donohue at Lincoln University (Pennsylvania). We especially want to recognize the work of Tiffany Temple, Legislative Assistant to Senator Sharon Weston Broome in Baton Rouge, Louisiana. In the first days of the project, State Senator Weston Broome saw the need for this project and put the resources of her office behind it.

We also want to thank all of those who contributed photographs for use in this collection. Special thanks go to Diane Elliott of University Photography Services, who made many of the photographs available to us, and the photographers who recorded pictorial diaries of each trip. All of these photographs were taken by James Madison University faculty, staff, and students who went on several hurricane-relief trips sponsored by the James Madison University Community Service Learning Office, College of Education, Wesley Foundation, and the Center for Multicultural Student Services since November 2005:

November 2005—Thanksgiving Hurricane Relief Trip to Biloxi, Mississippi
    Led by Dr. Mary Slade, Steve Atwell, Leah Goodman (54 participants)

Spring Break 2006 to Bogalusa, Louisiana
    Triangle of Hope led by Tami Parker, Kristen McDuffie (10 participants)

March 2006 to New Orleans, Louisiana
    Led by Center for Multicultural Student Services (23 participants)

May Hurricane Relief Trip 2006 to Waveland, Mississippi
    Dr. Mary Slade, Steve Atwell, Jill Treacy (56 participants)

March 2006 and 2007 to Moss Point, Mississippi
> Wesley Foundation at JMU led by Rev. Derrick Parson; photographer, Jess Hoffman (41 participants)

November 2006 to New Orleans, Louisiana
> College of Education sponsored trip led by Dr. Mary Slade and Jenn Schraw (110 participants)

Spring Break 2007 to New Orleans, Louisiana
> Mardi Gras Service Corps led by Brendan Sloan, Nicole Snyder (10 participants)

May Hurricane Relief Trip 2007 to New Orleans, Louisiana
> Heather Roberts, Lauren Caskey, Jenny Baker (54 participants)

November 2007 to New Orleans, Louisiana
        College of Education sponsored trip led by Dr. Mary
Slade and Justin Broughman; photographer, Kai Degner (108
participants)

Spring Break 2008
        Hands on Gulf Coast, Mississippi led by Brandi
Mooring and Chantee Brakeville (10 participants)

SAFER, New Orleans led by Jennifer Rowe, Emma Smith (10
participants)

May Hurricane Relief Trip 2008
        Jeremy Hawkins, Mark Bushy, Erin Kauffman (56
participants)

The number of trips and participants is a testament to James Madison University's national reputation for community service and the continuing need for assistance in this region.

This project was underwritten by the RR Donnelley Foundation, whose generous contribution has made the "My Soul Is Anchored" CD as well as this collection possible. I would like to thank Calvin Butler, formerly in the Office of External Affairs at RR Donnelley, for supporting this project. I would also like to acknowledge the generosity of my husband, Alexander Gabbin, who believed in this project from the very beginning and gave the initial seed money to launch it.

No project of this nature gets completed without the assistance and diligence of talented people. I want to thank my editorial assistants Julie Caran and Natalia Bradshaw Parson for an incredible job. They were dedicated to the vision and mission of this project and kept the project moving forward. I also want to thank Clarissa Shoecraft, Elizabeth Haworth and the entire Furious Flower Poetry Center staff for supporting and encouraging this project. I am grateful for the cooperation and professionalism of Andy Wolfe, Jennifer Young and the members of the staff at Mariner Media, Inc. for their assistance in publishing, designing, and marketing this volume.

About the Editor

Joanne V. Gabbin is Professor of English at James Madison University where she is Executive Director of the Furious Flower Poetry Center. She is author of *Sterling A. Brown: Building the Black Aesthetic Tradition,* editor of *Furious Flower: A Revolution in African American Poetry* and *The Furious Flowering of African American Poetry,* and executive producer of the Furious Flower video and DVD series.

A dedicated teacher and scholar, she has received numerous awards for excellence in teaching and scholarship. Among them are the College Language Association Creative Scholarship Award for her book Sterling A. Brown (1986), the James Madison University Faculty Women's Caucus and Women's Resource Network for Scholarship (1988), and the Outstanding Faculty Award, Virginia State Council of Higher Education.

Dr. Gabbin was the recipient of two faculty awards: the Provost's Award for Distinguished Service and the JMU Alumni Distinguished Faculty Award. In 2005, Dr. Gabbin was inducted into the International Literary Hall of Fame for Writers of African Descent. She is also founder and organizer of the Wintergreen Women Writers' Collective, owner of the 150 Franklin Street Gallery in Harrisonburg, and author of the children's book *I Bet She Called Me Sugar Plum.*